Tomoko Fuse's
ORIGAMI BOXES

TUTTLE Publishing

Tokyo | Rutland, Vermont | Singapore

Contents

Note on Size References—for each project we have indicated the dimensions
of the finished box. These measurements are for your reference.

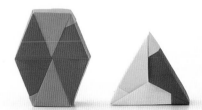

Box size 2 x 2 in {5 x 5 cm}   Box size 6 x 6 in {15 x 15 cm}

Part 2
Modular Boxes From Multiple Square Sheets

Part 3
Modular Boxes From Rectangular Sheets

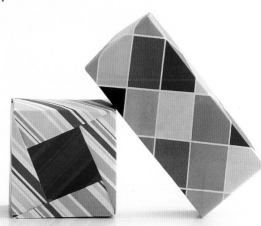

A Guide to Origami Symbols and Basic Folds

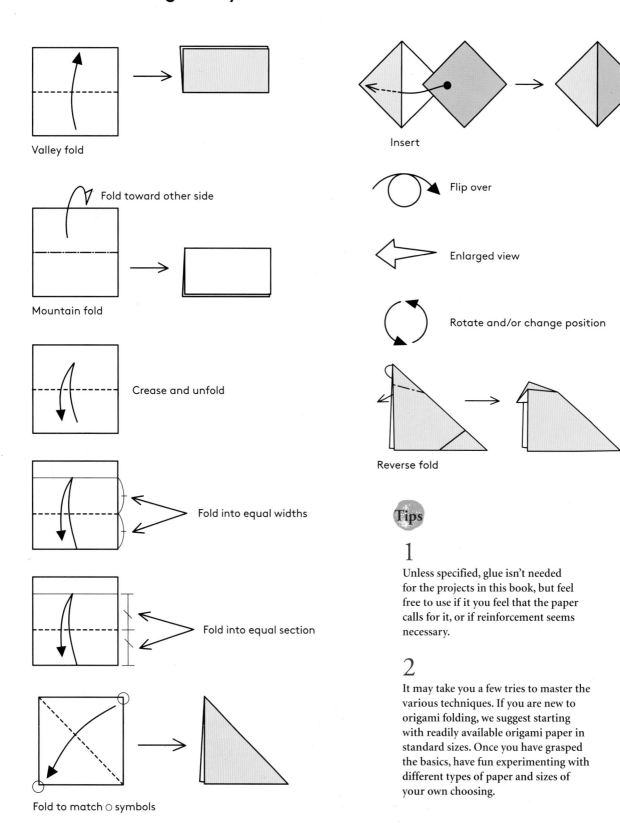

Valley fold

Fold toward other side

Mountain fold

Crease and unfold

Fold into equal widths

Fold into equal section

Fold to match ○ symbols

Insert

Flip over

Enlarged view

Rotate and/or change position

Reverse fold

Tips

1

Unless specified, glue isn't needed for the projects in this book, but feel free to use if it you feel that the paper calls for it, or if reinforcement seems necessary.

2

It may take you a few tries to master the various techniques. If you are new to origami folding, we suggest starting with readily available origami paper in standard sizes. Once you have grasped the basics, have fun experimenting with different types of paper and sizes of your own choosing.

Part 1
Simple Boxes From Square Sheets

The base and lid for each box are each folded from a single square sheet of paper. Both are very easy to make. Practice first with commercially-available, standard-sized origami paper, then try your hand at varying the sizes and using some of your favorite specialty papers. The simpler the design, the more the paper will shine.

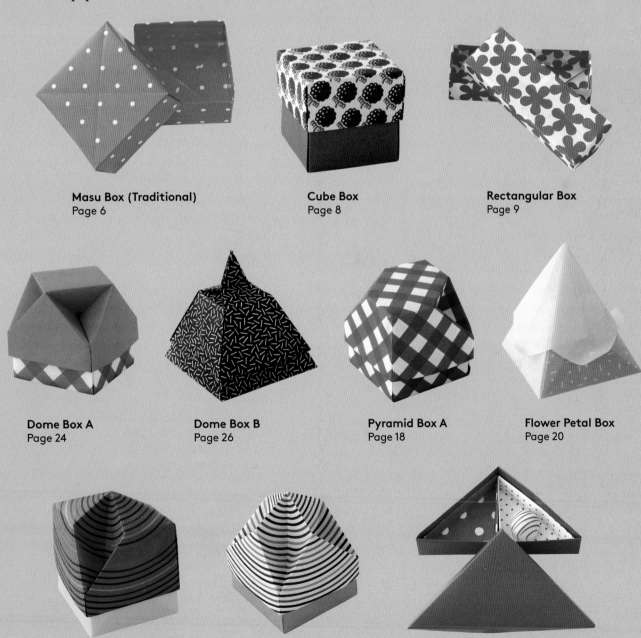

Masu Box (Traditional)
Page 6

Cube Box
Page 8

Rectangular Box
Page 9

Dome Box A
Page 24

Dome Box B
Page 26

Pyramid Box A
Page 18

Flower Petal Box
Page 20

Dome Box D
Page 27

Dome Box C
Page 27

Triangular Box with Internal Partitions
Page 14

The Traditional Masu Box
6 x 6 in (15 x 15 cm) sheets are standard

The traditional "Masu" box is folded from a square sheet of paper and has many variations. Let's start with the basics.

Basic Masu Base

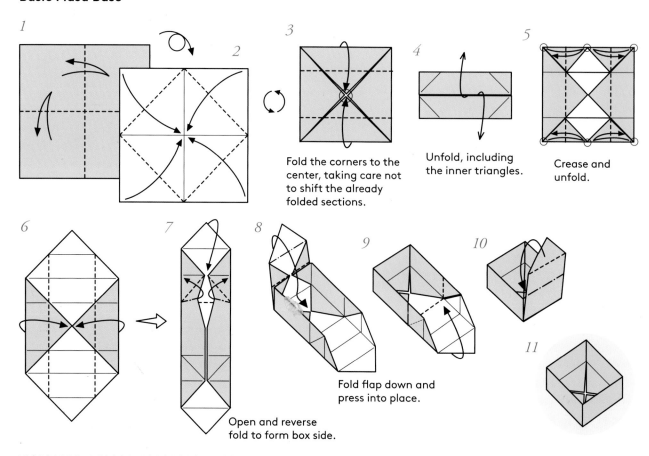

3 Fold the corners to the center, taking care not to shift the already folded sections.

4 Unfold, including the inner triangles.

5 Crease and unfold.

7 Open and reverse fold to form box side.

8 Fold flap down and press into place.

Masu Variation 1
Square Box with a Lid 6 x 6 in (15 x 15 cm) sheets are standard

To make a lid for the Masa Box above, start from step 3 of the Basic Masu Base instructions:

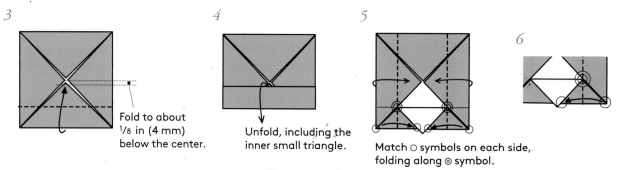

3 Fold to about 1/8 in (4 mm) below the center.

4 Unfold, including the inner small triangle.

5 Match ○ symbols on each side, folding along ◎ symbol.

6

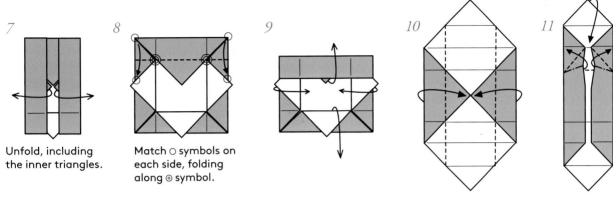

7

Unfold, including the inner triangles.

8

Match ○ symbols on each side, folding along ◎ symbol.

9

10

11

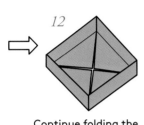

12

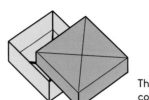

Continue folding the rest of the box using steps 7-11 from page 6.

The box is now complete.

Tip By changing the width of the folds, you can vary the box dimensions

2¹/₈ x 2¹/₈ x 1 in
(5.25 x 5.25 x 2.5 cm)

Cube Box with a Lid 6 x 6 in (15 x 15 cm) sheets are standard

Because this style of Masu Box will be deeper, it will work well for the base of the Dome Box (page 24)

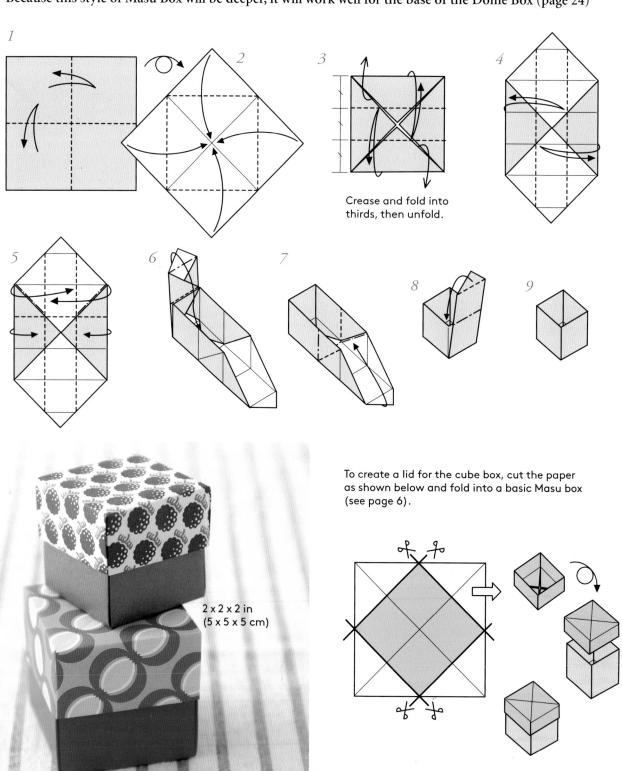

Crease and fold into thirds, then unfold.

2 x 2 x 2 in (5 x 5 x 5 cm)

To create a lid for the cube box, cut the paper as shown below and fold into a basic Masu box (see page 6).

Masu Variation 3
Rectangular Box 6 x 6 in (15 x 15 cm) sheets are standard

Now let's modify the Masu into a rectangular box. This method was created by origami artist Hisashi Abe; in this variation we've added steps to include a lid.

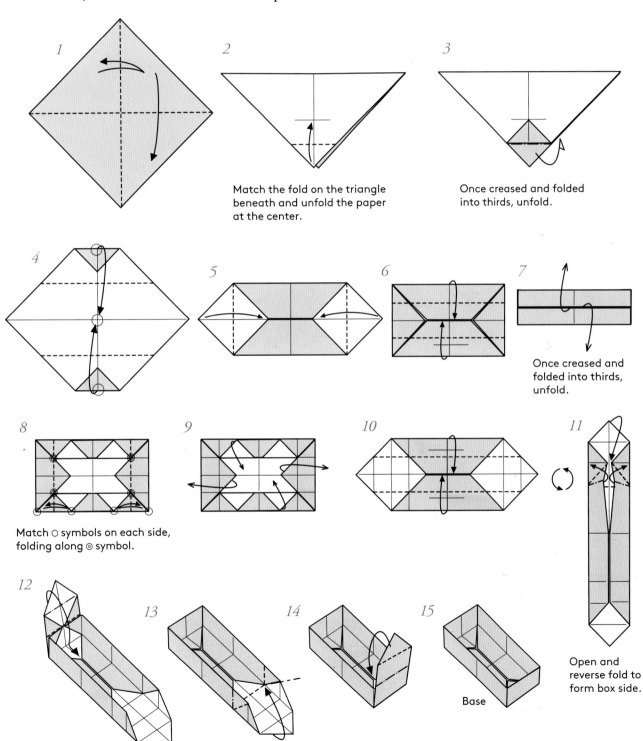

2 Match the fold on the triangle beneath and unfold the paper at the center.

3 Once creased and folded into thirds, unfold.

7 Once creased and folded into thirds, unfold.

8 Match ○ symbols on each side, folding along ◎ symbol.

11 Open and reverse fold to form box side.

15 Base

Masu Variation 4
Rectangular Box with a Lid 6 x 6 in (15 x 15 cm) sheets are standard

Start from step 6 on page 9.

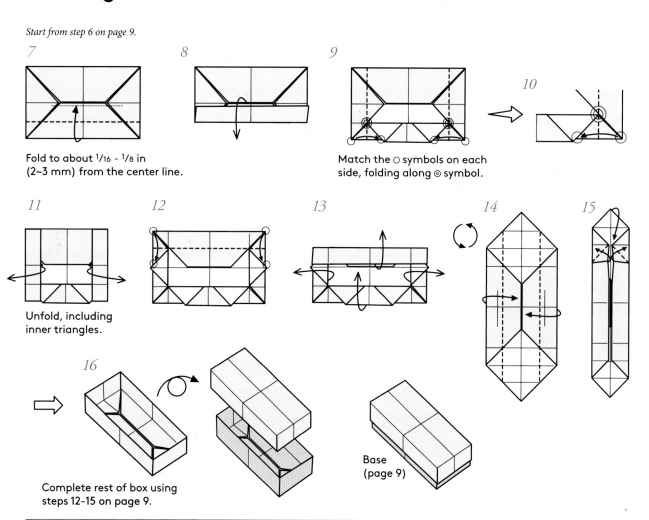

7

Fold to about 1/16 - 1/8 in (2~3 mm) from the center line.

8

9

Match the ○ symbols on each side, folding along ◉ symbol.

10

11

Unfold, including inner triangles.

12

13

14

15

16

Complete rest of box using steps 12-15 on page 9.

Base (page 9)

How to Determine the depth of the box   **Tip**   The depth of the box is determined by the width of the fold from step 2 on page 9. The basic square Masu box does not include this fold. By increasing this fold, the shape become a thinner rectangle.

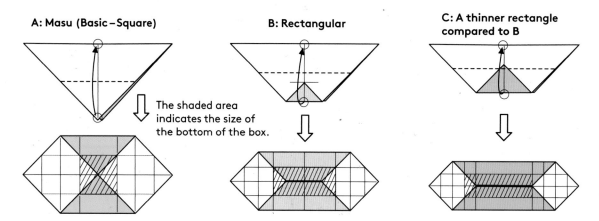

A: Masu (Basic – Square)

B: Rectangular

C: A thinner rectangle compared to B

The shaded area indicates the size of the bottom of the box.

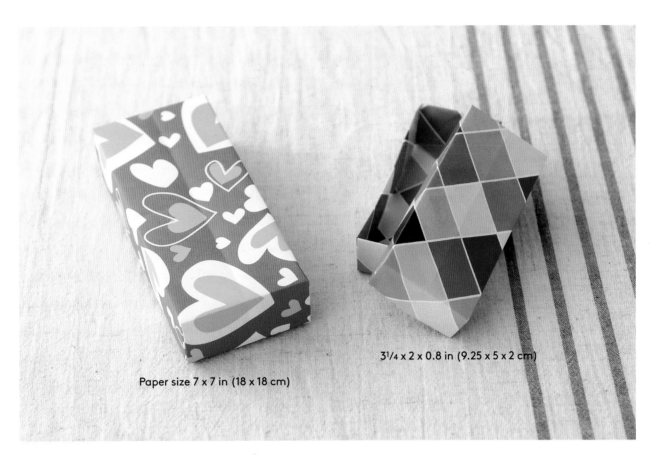

3¹/₄ x 2 x 0.8 in (9.25 x 5 x 2 cm)

Paper size 7 x 7 in (18 x 18 cm)

Masu Variation 5
A Masu Box with a Window 6 x 6 in (15 x 15 cm) sheets are standard

A diamond-shaped opening is the main feature of this box.
You can also create a lid out of a basic Masu box by matching the dimensions of the base.

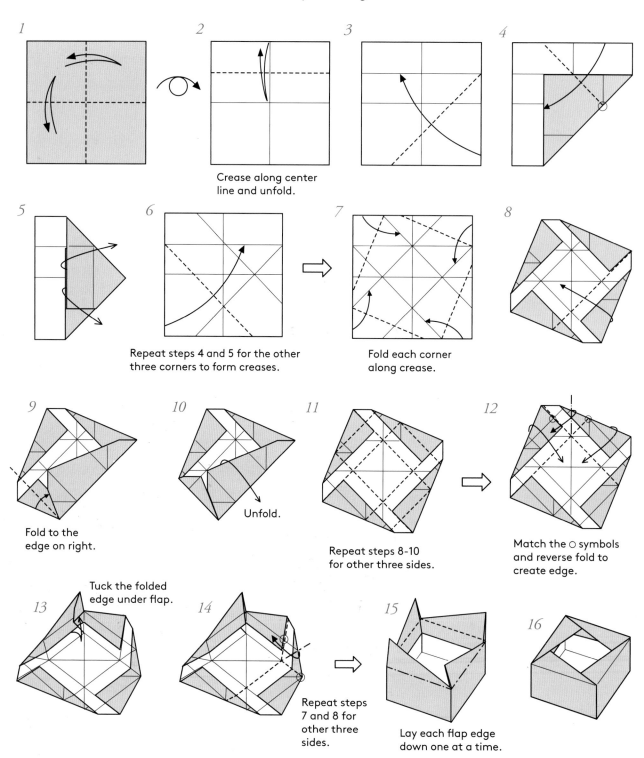

1

2
Crease along center
line and unfold.

3

4

5

6
Repeat steps 4 and 5 for the other
three corners to form creases.

7
Fold each corner
along crease.

8

9
Fold to the
edge on right.

10
Unfold.

11
Repeat steps 8-10
for other three sides.

12
Match the ○ symbols
and reverse fold to
create edge.

13
Tuck the folded
edge under flap.

14
Repeat steps
7 and 8 for
other three
sides.

15
Lay each flap edge
down one at a time.

16

How to Change the depth The fold from step 2 on page 14 determines the depth of the box. The fold line in version A produces a very shallow box. Folding above this line, as in version B, will increase the depth of the box.

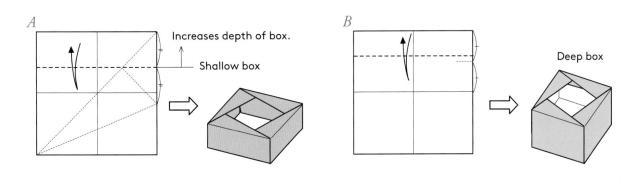

A

Increases depth of box.

Shallow box

B

Deep box

Paper size
8 1/4 x 8 1/4 in (21 x 21 cm)

2 1/8 x 2 1/8 x 1 1/8 in
(5.5 x 5.5 x 3 cm)

Triangular Box with Internal Partitions

6 x 6 in (15 x 15 cm) sheets are standard

To make the lid, increase the width of the fold in step 2. By adjusting this fold you can create nesting boxes.

Box A (Basic Triangular Box)

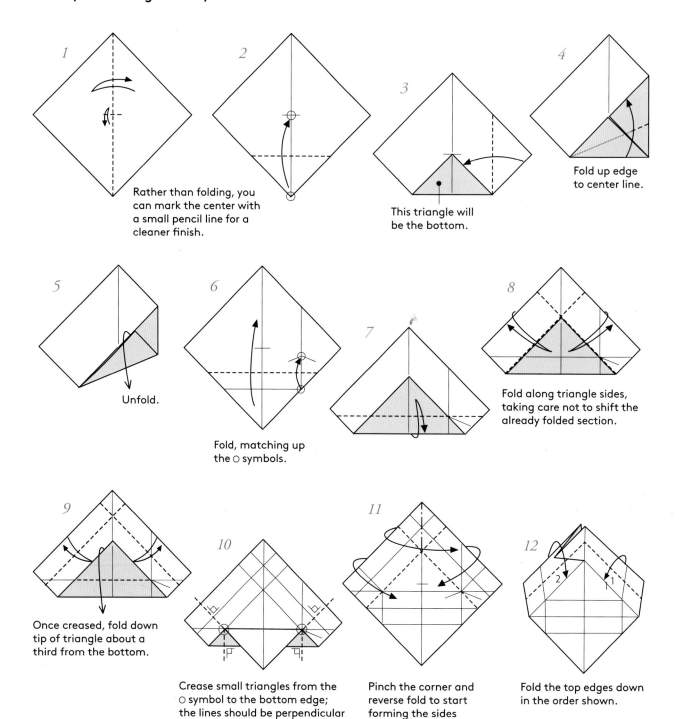

1

Rather than folding, you can mark the center with a small pencil line for a cleaner finish.

2

3

This triangle will be the bottom.

4

Fold up edge to center line.

5

Unfold.

6

Fold, matching up the ○ symbols.

7

8

Fold along triangle sides, taking care not to shift the already folded section.

9

Once creased, fold down tip of triangle about a third from the bottom.

10

Crease small triangles from the ○ symbol to the bottom edge; the lines should be perpendicular to the bottom edge.

11

Pinch the corner and reverse fold to start forming the sides

12

Fold the top edges down in the order shown.

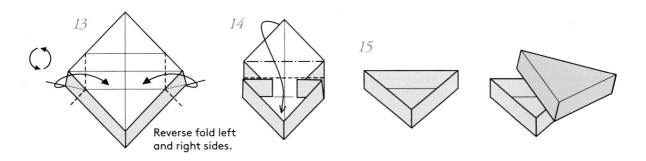

13

14

15

Reverse fold left
and right sides.

Larger and shallower than Box A: The lid for for Box A

Tip Helpful dimensions for creating lids
For 6 x 6 in (15 x 15 cm) paper, fold about $1/4$ - $3/8$ in
(0.8 cm) above the center line.

For $10^{1}/4$ x $10^{1}/4$ in (26 x 26 cm) paper, fold about $5/8$ in
(1.5 cm) above the center line.

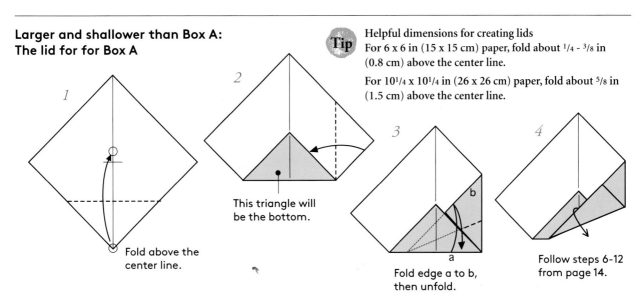

1

Fold above the
center line.

2

This triangle will
be the bottom.

3

b

a

Fold edge a to b,
then unfold.

4

Follow steps 6-12
from page 14.

Paper size for large box
$10^{1}/4$ x $10^{1}/4$ in (26 x 26 cm)

Shallower and smaller than box A: Lid for box A

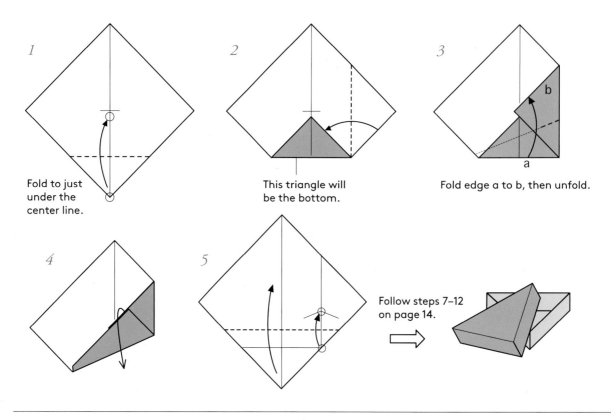

1

Fold to just under the center line.

2

This triangle will be the bottom.

3

Fold edge a to b, then unfold.

4

5

Follow steps 7–12 on page 14.

Masu Variation 6

A (Basic)

Refer to the dimensions below to make the partition boxes. Decreasing the dimensions ¹/₁₆ in (3 mm) for the medium size and keeping the same length for both the small and medium sizes seem to allow the best fit within the base. However, fit can differ depending on the paper thickness and box size, so test out a few practice partition boxes before folding the final versions.

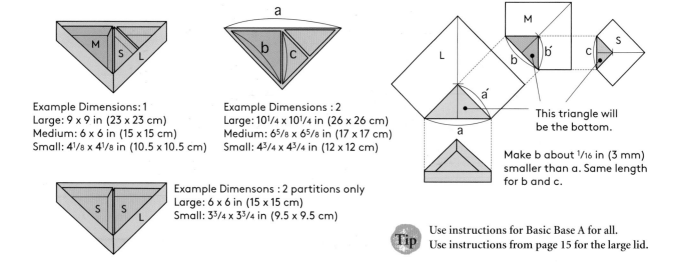

Example Dimensions: 1
Large: 9 x 9 in (23 x 23 cm)
Medium: 6 x 6 in (15 x 15 cm)
Small: 4¹/₈ x 4¹/₈ in (10.5 x 10.5 cm)

Example Dimensions : 2
Large: 10¹/₄ x 10¹/₄ in (26 x 26 cm)
Medium: 6⁵/₈ x 6⁵/₈ in (17 x 17 cm)
Small: 4³/₄ x 4³/₄ in (12 x 12 cm)

Example Dimensons : 2 partitions only
Large: 6 x 6 in (15 x 15 cm)
Small: 3³/₄ x 3³/₄ in (9.5 x 9.5 cm)

This triangle will be the bottom.

Make b about ¹/₁₆ in (3 mm) smaller than a. Same length for b and c.

Tip Use instructions for Basic Base A for all. Use instructions from page 15 for the large lid.

One large triangle, two medium triangles

One large triangle, one medium triangle, two small triangles

Pyramid Boxes 6 x 6 in (15 x 15 cm) sheets are standard

In this section you'll learn how to make a pyramid-shaped box with a pointy tip.

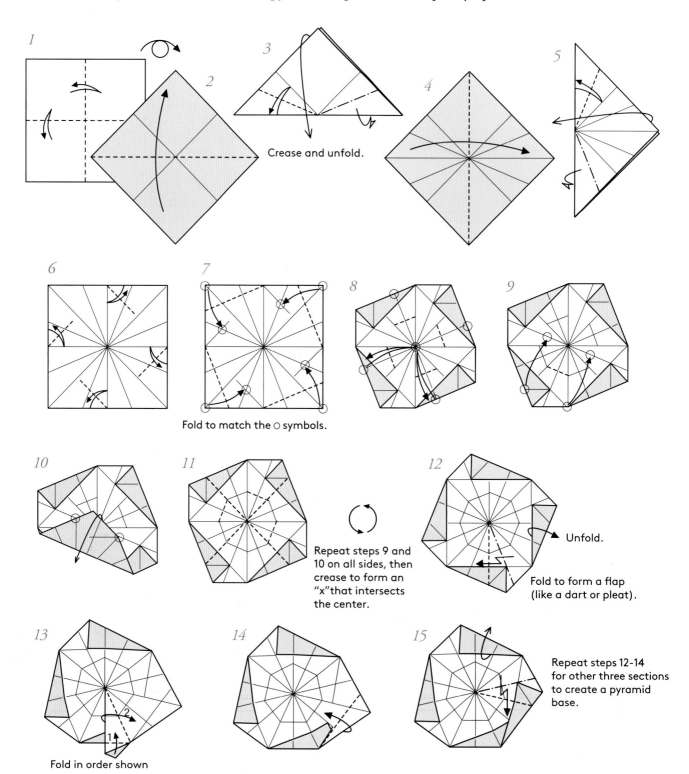

1

2

3

Crease and unfold.

4

5

6

7

Fold to match the ○ symbols.

8

9

10

11

Repeat steps 9 and 10 on all sides, then crease to form an "x" that intersects the center.

12

Unfold.

Fold to form a flap (like a dart or pleat).

13

Fold in order shown

14

15

Repeat steps 12-14 for other three sections to create a pyramid base.

16

17

Fold and tuck beneath flap.

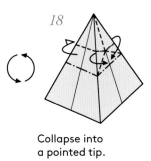
18

Collapse into
a pointed tip.

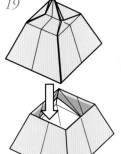
19

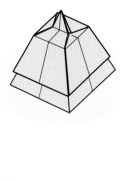

Base (page 22)

Variation [B] from step 17

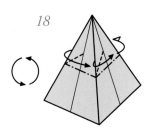
18

Twist to form pointed tip.

19

Base (Page 22)

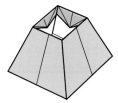

Pyramid Box 2¼ x 2¼ x 1¾ in
(5.75 x 5.75 x 4.5 cm)
(height does not include pointed tip).

Flower Petal Box 6 x 6 in (15 x 15 cm) sheets are standard

The pyramid-shaped lid will be arranged into a flower.

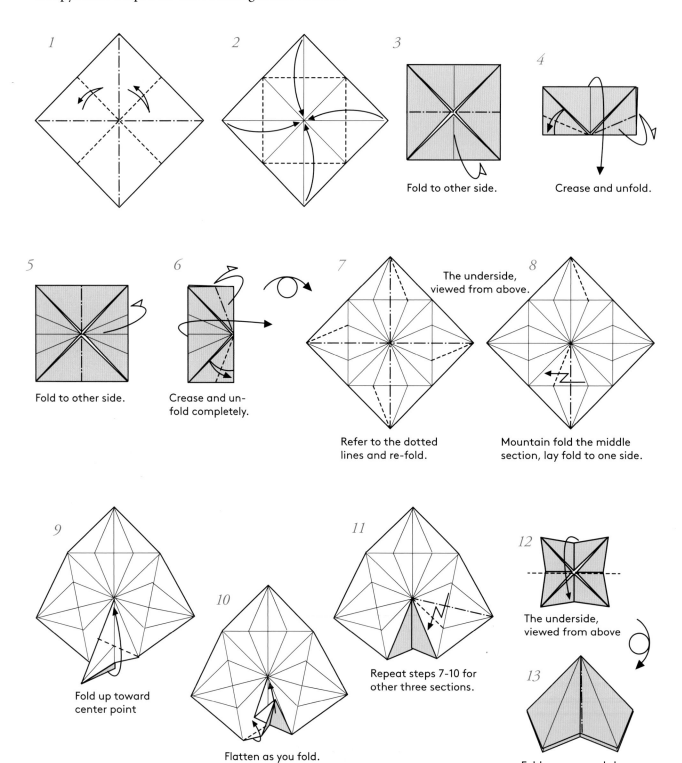

1

2

3

Fold to other side.

4

Crease and unfold.

5

Fold to other side.

6

Crease and un-
fold completely.

7

The underside,
viewed from above.

Refer to the dotted
lines and re-fold.

8

Mountain fold the middle
section, lay fold to one side.

9

Fold up toward
center point

10

Flatten as you fold.

11

Repeat steps 7–10 for
other three sections.

12

The underside,
viewed from above

13

Fold creases and shape
into a pyramid.

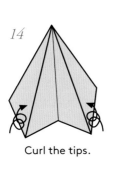

14

Curl the tips.

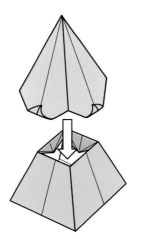

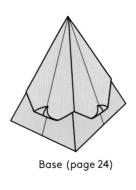

Base (page 24)

Deep Base 2¹/₄ x 2¹/₄ x 2³/₄ in
(5.75 x 5.75 x 7 cm)

Pyramid Box Base 6 x 6 in (15 x 15 cm) sheets are standard

A few changes in the early steps will yield a deeper base. An insert reinforces the bottom.

Shallow Base

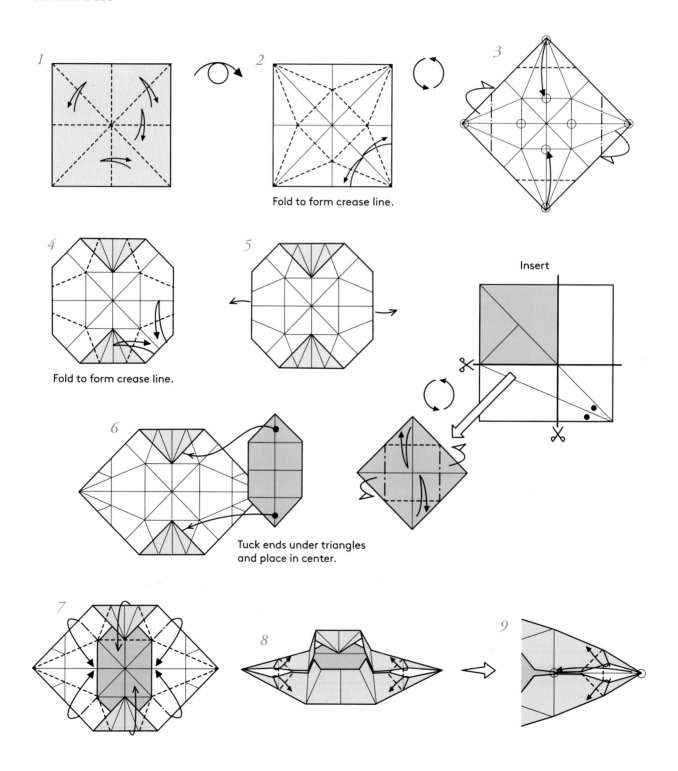

2
Fold to form crease line.

4
Fold to form crease line.

Insert

6
Tuck ends under triangles and place in center.

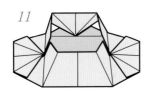

10

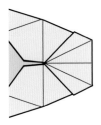

11

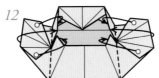

12

13

To strengthen the box,
attach glue where indicated.

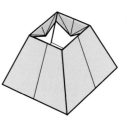

Deep Base from step 3 on page 22

3

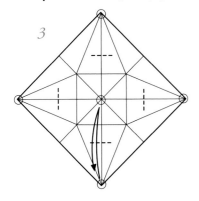

4

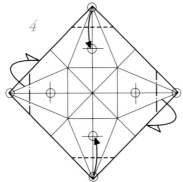

Complete the rest
of the box using
steps 4-13 on
pages 22 and 23.

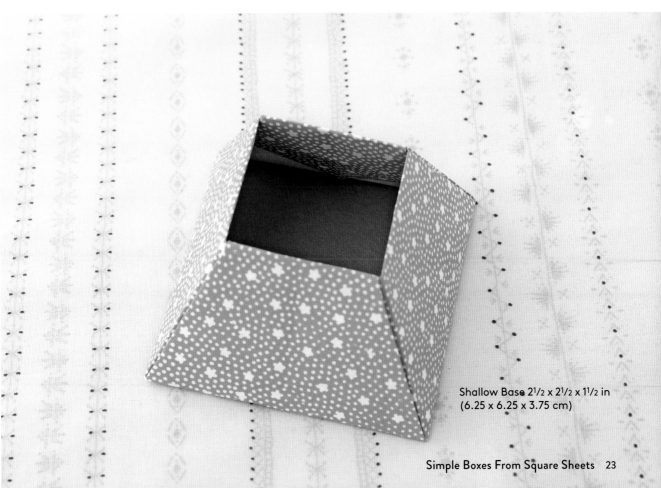

Shallow Base 2¹/₂ x 2¹/₂ x 1¹/₂ in
(6.25 x 6.25 x 3.75 cm)

Dome Box A 6 x 6 in (15 x 15 cm) sheets are standard

Bumpy, geometric crenulations are the highlights of this dome-shaped lid. The insert is key to reinforcing the paper and streamlining the appearance of the lid interior. The base is the traditional Masu box.

Lid : A **Tip** If you can, try to avoid folding the cross section enclosed within the circle in step 1 for both A and B lids. This results in a cleaner finish without excess lines.

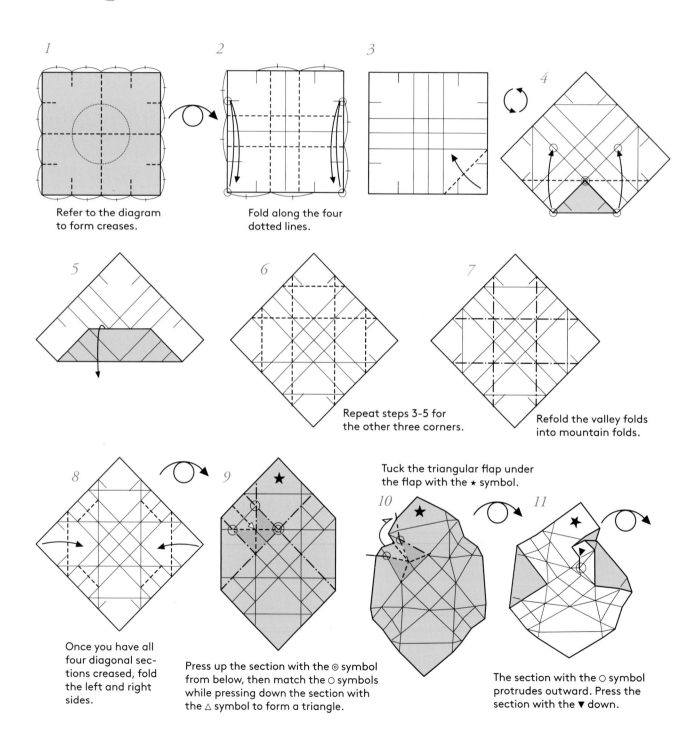

1

Refer to the diagram to form creases.

2

Fold along the four dotted lines.

3

4

5

6

Repeat steps 3-5 for the other three corners.

7

Refold the valley folds into mountain folds.

8

Once you have all four diagonal sections creased, fold the left and right sides.

9

Press up the section with the ⊚ symbol from below, then match the ○ symbols while pressing down the section with the △ symbol to form a triangle.

Tuck the triangular flap under the flap with the ★ symbol.

10

11

The section with the ○ symbol protrudes outward. Press the section with the ▼ down.

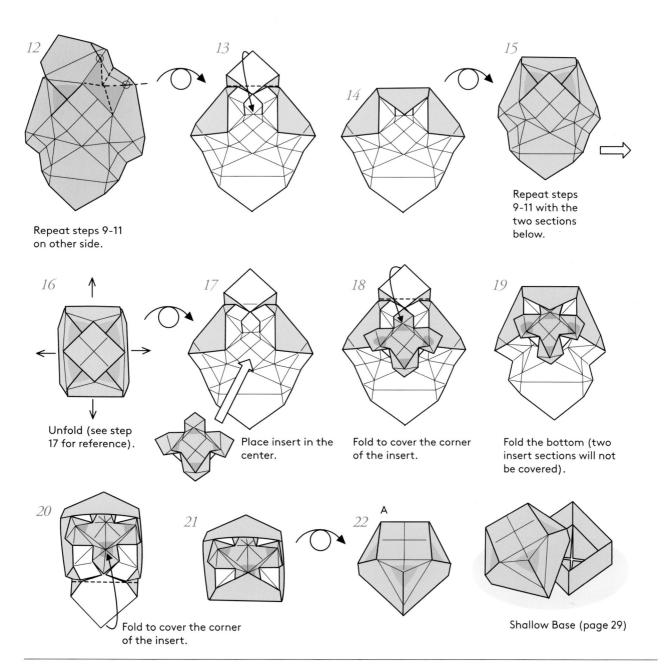

12 Repeat steps 9-11 on other side.

13

14

15 Repeat steps 9-11 with the two sections below.

16 Unfold (see step 17 for reference).

17 Place insert in the center.

18 Fold to cover the corner of the insert.

19 Fold the bottom (two insert sections will not be covered).

20 Fold to cover the corner of the insert.

21

22 A

Shallow Base (page 29)

Insert

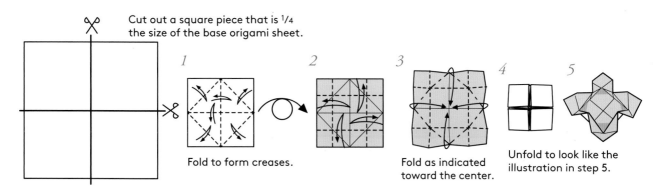

Cut out a square piece that is 1/4 the size of the base origami sheet.

1 Fold to form creases.

2

3 Fold as indicated toward the center.

4

5 Unfold to look like the illustration in step 5.

Dome Box B 6 x 6 in (15 x 15 cm) sheets are standard

For A, all the corners were pressed in; for this version, however, we'll do the reverse for all but one corner.

From step 11 on page 24

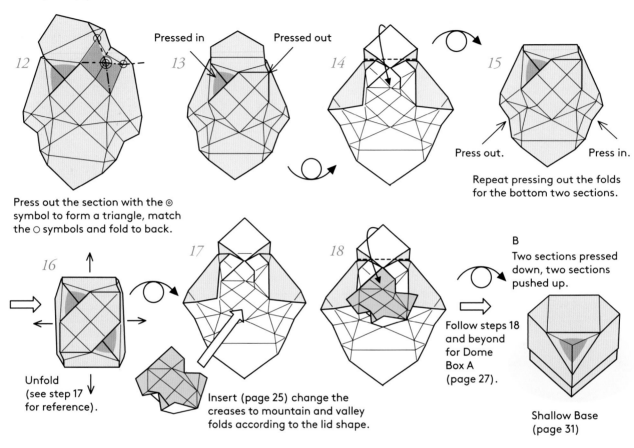

12

13 Pressed in   Pressed out

14

15 Press out.   Press in.

Repeat pressing out the folds for the bottom two sections.

Press out the section with the ◎ symbol to form a triangle, match the ○ symbols and fold to back.

16

Unfold (see step 17 for reference).

17

Insert (page 25) change the creases to mountain and valley folds according to the lid shape.

18

Follow steps 18 and beyond for Dome Box A (page 27).

B Two sections pressed down, two sections pushed up.

Shallow Base (page 31)

Dome Box C and D 6 x 6 in (15 x 15 cm) sheets are standard

Starting with step 8 for Dome Box A (page 24)

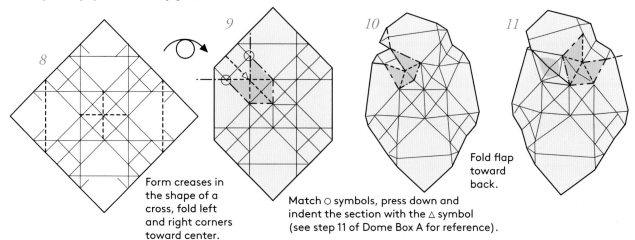

8

9

Form creases in the shape of a cross, fold left and right corners toward center.

10

11

Match ○ symbols, press down and indent the section with the △ symbol (see step 11 of Dome Box A for reference).

Fold flap toward back.

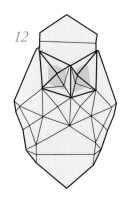

12

Repeat with other two sections.

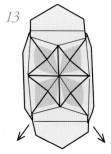

13

Unfold the bottom two sections.

Continues on page 28

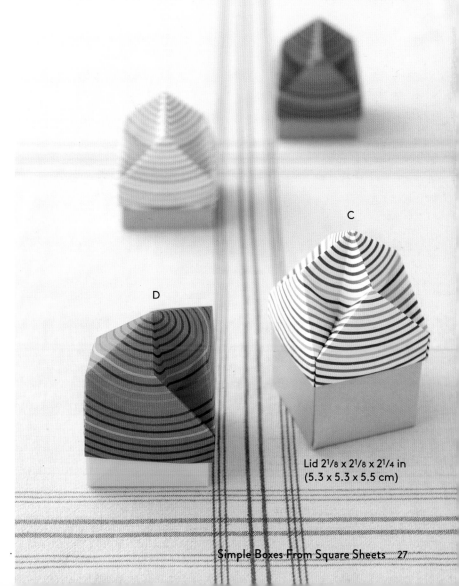

D

C

Lid 2¹/₈ x 2¹/₈ x 2¹/₄ in (5.3 x 5.3 x 5.5 cm)

Continued from page 27

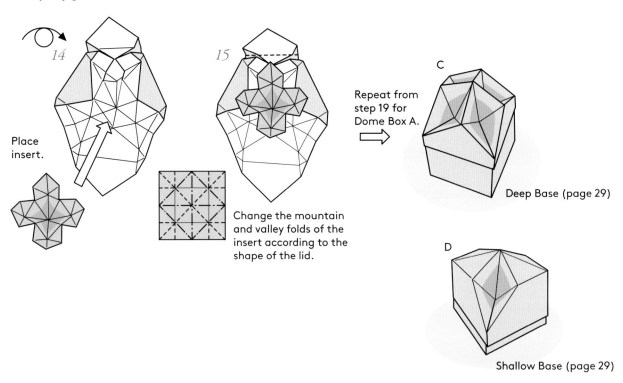

14

Place insert.

15

Change the mountain and valley folds of the insert according to the shape of the lid.

Repeat from step 19 for Dome Box A.

C

Deep Base (page 29)

D

Shallow Base (page 29)

C

D

A

B

Lid 2 ¹/₁₆ x 2 ¹/₁₆ x 1¹/₈ in
(5.25 x 5.25 x 3.5 cm)

Dome Box Base 6 x 6 in (15 x 15 cm) sheets are standard

Use the Masu box for the Dome Box base

Shallow Base: Masu

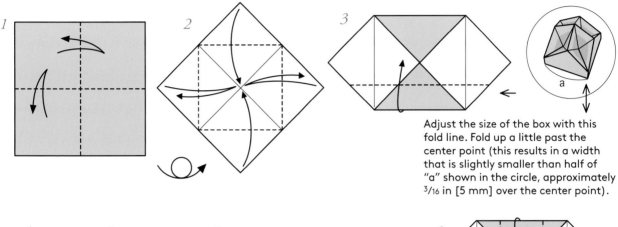

Adjust the size of the box with this fold line. Fold up a little past the center point (this results in a width that is slightly smaller than half of "a" shown in the circle, approximately $^3/_{16}$ in [5 mm] over the center point).

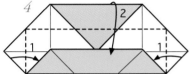

Fold in the order shown.

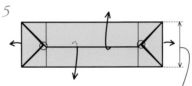

Smaller than "a". This width is the size of the box bottom.

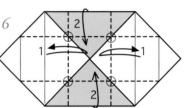

Crease the dotted lines labeled 1 unfold, then fold dotted lines labeled 2.

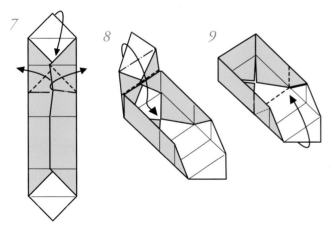

Dimensions to increase the depth of the base

The Cube Base is folded from a sheet 1.4 times the size of the paper used for the Dome Box.

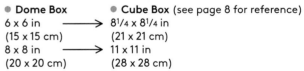

● **Dome Box**
6 x 6 in
(15 x 15 cm)
8 x 8 in
(20 x 20 cm)

● **Cube Box** (see page 8 for reference)
8¹/₄ x 8¹/₄ in
(21 x 21 cm)
11 x 11 in
(28 x 28 cm)

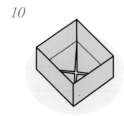

Shallow Base

Deep Base

Part 2
Modular Boxes From Multiple Square Sheets

"Modular Origami" involves folding multiple pieces of paper in the same way and assembling them together into a box. In addition to triangular, square, rectangular, hexagonal and other polygonal shapes, we've included fun options that look like bento boxes, barrels and more. Modular boxes can be combined in lots creative and imaginative ways!

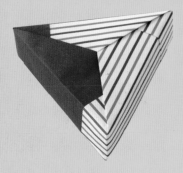

Triangular Box • *Tomoe*
Page 32

Square Box • *Hanabishi*
Page 41

Square Box • *Yaehanabishi*
Page 42

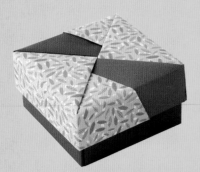

Square Box • *Suehiro*
(***Kongo-gumi*** [Spiral Braid])
Page 40

Square Box • *Suehiro*
(***Chomusubi*** [Butterfly Knot])
Page 37

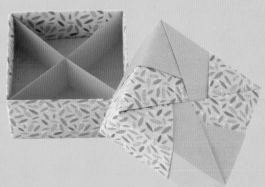

Square Box • *Suehiro*
(***Manji*** Pattern)
Page 38

"X" Partition
Page 45

Flower Roll Box • A
Page 46

Flower Roll Box • D
Page 48

Flower Roll Spiral Box
Page 50

Rectangular Box
Page 60

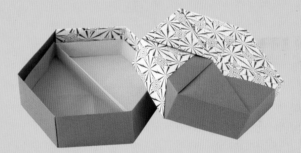

Hexagonal Box—3 sheet assembly • Plain 2
Page 55

Half Hexagonal Box
Page 58

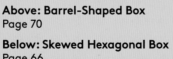

Above: Barrel-Shaped Box
Page 70

Below: Skewed Hexagonal Box
Page 66

Hexagonal Box—3 sheet assembly • Pansy 1
Page 52

Modular *Tomoe* Triangular Box Base and Lid 6 x 6 in (15 x 15 cm) sheets are standard

Create the base and lid from paper that is the same size

To use different-sized paper:
Large: 4⁷/₈ x 4¹/₈ x 1¹/₄ in (12.3 x 10.5 x 3.3 cm)
(Origami 6 x 6 in [15 x 15 cm])

Small: 1⁵/₈ x 1³/₈ x ¹/₂ in (4 x 3.5 x 1.2 cm)
(Origami 2 x 2 in [5 x 5 cm])

Base

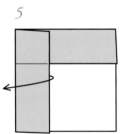

1

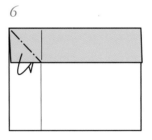

2

3

4

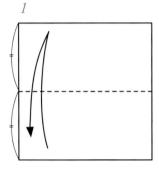

5

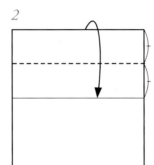

6

Fold the triangular corner under.

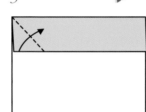

7

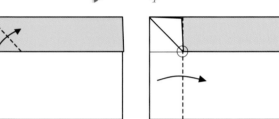

8

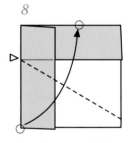

Starting at △ fold along dotted line to match the ○ symbols.

9

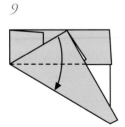

10

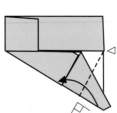

Starting at △ fold along dotted line, keeping edges aligned.

11

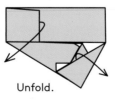

Unfold.

12

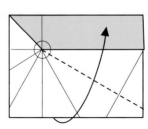

From the ○ symbol fold up along dotted line.

13

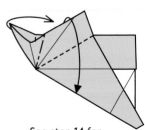

See step 14 for reference.

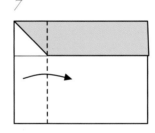
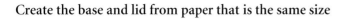

14

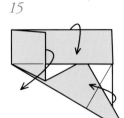

Tuck in the section
with the ○ symbol.

15

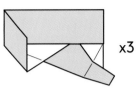

Bring sides forward.

16

Lift the edge and prop up
the right section.

x3

Assembly

First, connect two pieces.

1

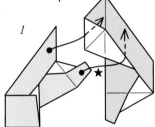

Insert the section with the
★ symbol into the second
piece, locking it in.

2

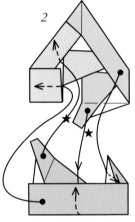

Third piece

3

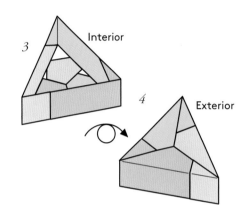

Interior

4

Exterior

Lid

1

Fold up approximately
to the center.

2

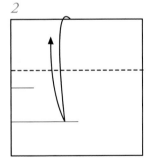

3

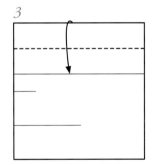

4

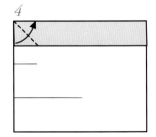

5

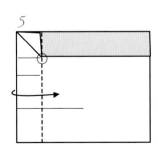

6

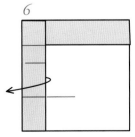

Unfold.

7

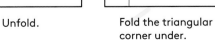

Fold the triangular
corner under.

Continues on page 34

Continued from page 33

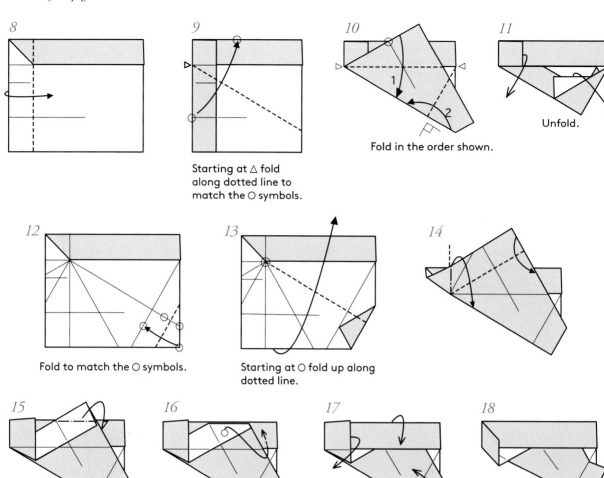

8

9

Starting at △ fold
along dotted line to
match the ○ symbols.

10

Fold in the order shown.

11

Unfold.

12

Fold to match the ○ symbols.

13

Starting at ○ fold up along
dotted line.

14

15

Fold along edge.

16

Tuck in section
with ○ symbol.

17

Bring sides
forwardl.

Lift the edge and prop up
the right section.

18

x 3

 Interior

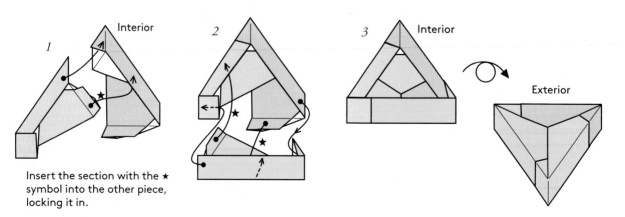

1

Interior

Insert the section with the ★
symbol into the other piece,
locking it in.

2

3

Interior

Exterior

3¹/₂ x 3¹/₂ x 1¹/₂ in
(11.3 x 11.3 x 3.7 cm)

Modular *Suehiro* Square Box and Lid

6 x 6 in (15 x 15 cm) sheets are standard

A square box made from four sheets. All the projects in this chapter are folded using a 6-in (15 cm) square sheet. Try mixing colors and prints.

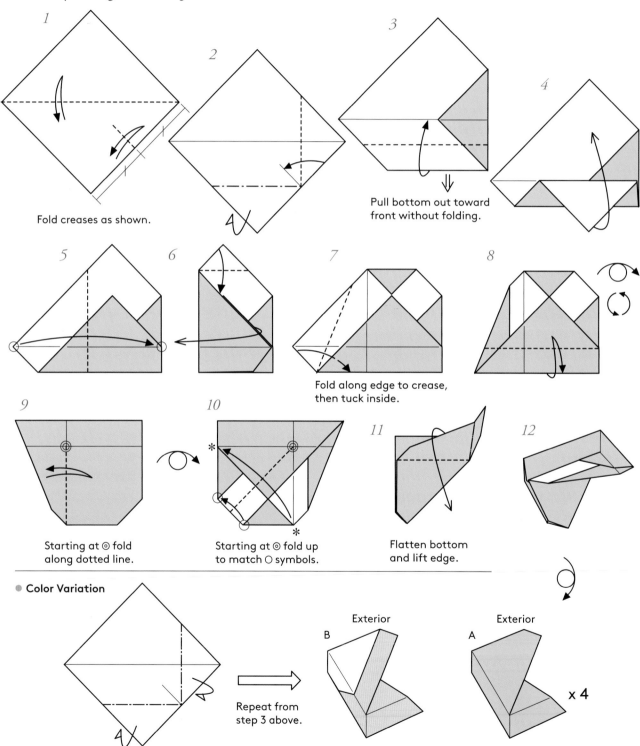

1

Fold creases as shown.

2

3

Pull bottom out toward front without folding.

4

5

6

7

Fold along edge to crease, then tuck inside.

8

9

Starting at ⊙ fold along dotted line.

10

Starting at ⊙ fold up to match ○ symbols.

11

Flatten bottom and lift edge.

12

● **Color Variation**

Repeat from step 3 above.

B Exterior

A Exterior

x 4

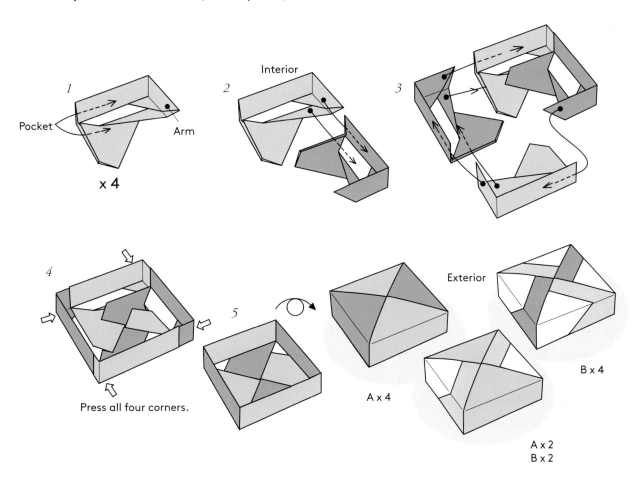

1

Pocket

Arm

x 4

2 Interior

3

4

Press all four corners.

5

A x 4

Exterior

B x 4

A x 2
B x 2

Hand positions for reference

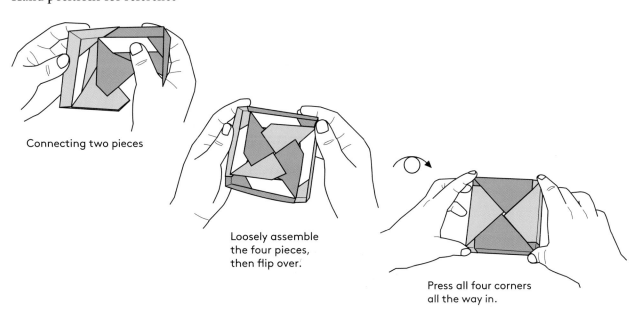

Connecting two pieces

Loosely assemble
the four pieces,
then flip over.

Press all four corners
all the way in.

Reverse the arm and pocket from Assembly Method 1.

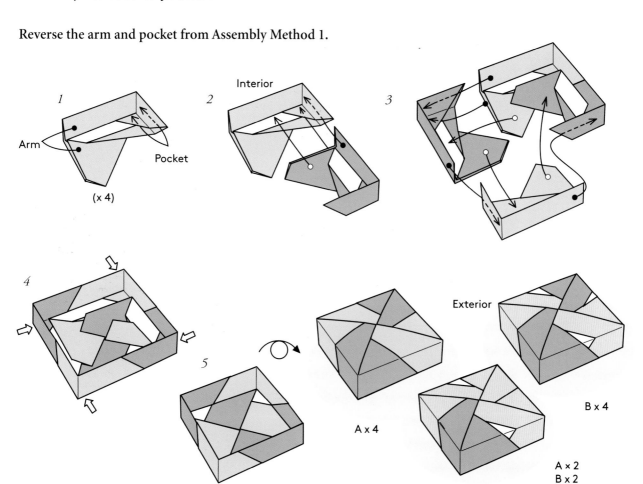

1

Arm

Pocket

(x 4)

2 Interior

3

4

5

Exterior

A x 4

B x 4

A × 2
B × 2

Hand positions for reference

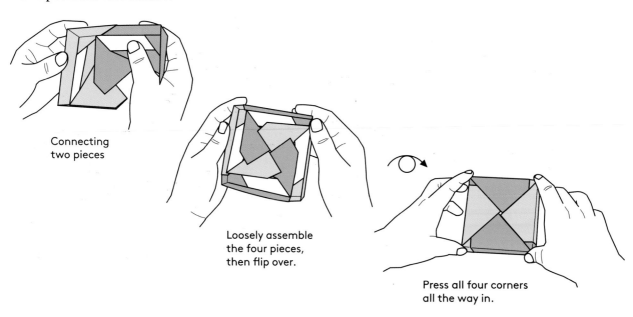

Connecting
two pieces

Loosely assemble
the four pieces,
then flip over.

Press all four corners
all the way in.

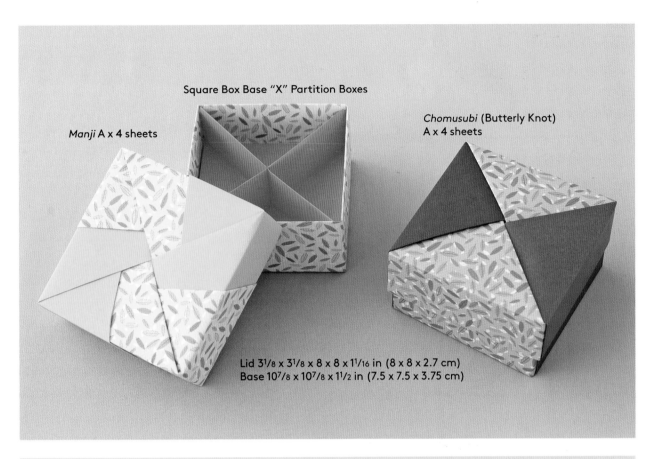

Square Box Base "X" Partition Boxes

Manji A x 4 sheets

Chomusubi (Butterly Knot)
A x 4 sheets

Lid 3$^{1}/_{8}$ x 3$^{1}/_{8}$ x 8 x 8 x 1$^{1}/_{16}$ in (8 x 8 x 2.7 cm)
Base 10$^{7}/_{8}$ x 10$^{7}/_{8}$ x 1$^{1}/_{2}$ in (7.5 x 7.5 x 3.75 cm)

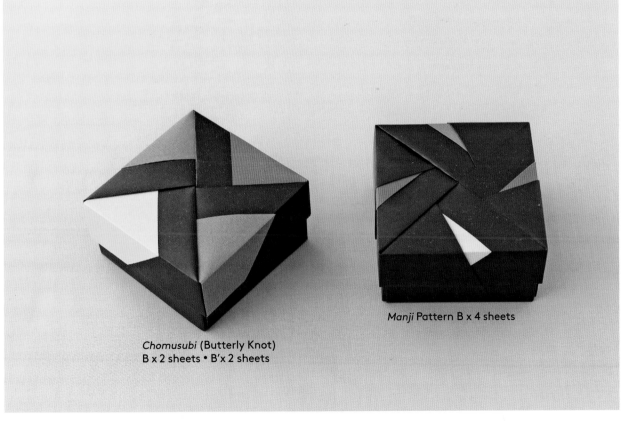

Chomusubi (Butterly Knot)
B x 2 sheets • B'x 2 sheets

Manji Pattern B x 4 sheets

● *Kongo-gumi* **(Spiral Braid)**

As shown below, this unit has pockets on both sides so pieces can be inserted on either side.
Use different colored/patterned sheets to make unique combinations.

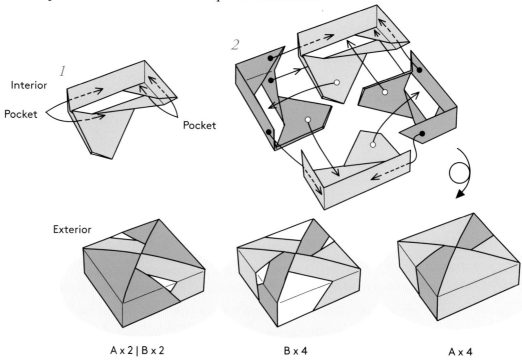

1

Interior

Pocket

Pocket

2

Exterior

A x 2 | B x 2   B x 4   A x 4

Kongo-gumi A x 2 sheets • B x 2 sheets

Kongo-gumi A x 4 sheets

Modular *Hanabishi* Square Box and Lid

6 x 6 in (15 x 15 cm) sheets are standard

Bend the tips of the *Hanabishi* petals for variation

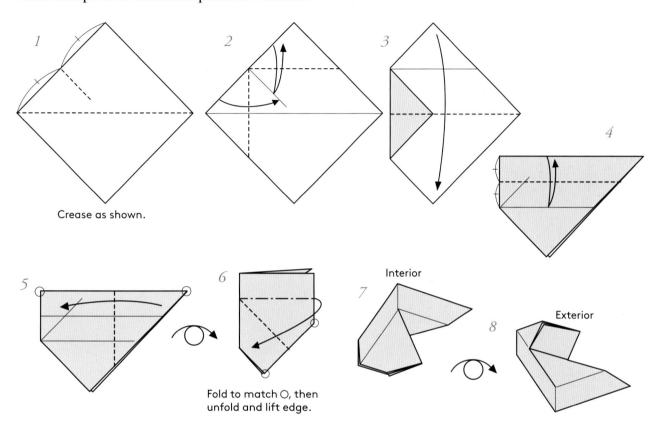

1 Crease as shown.

2

3

4

5

6 Fold to match ○, then unfold and lift edge.

7 Interior

8 Exterior

● **Assembly**

Shown: interior and exterior of the same two pieces

Loosely assemble the four pieces, then tighten securely together by pushing all the way in (see page 37 for reference).

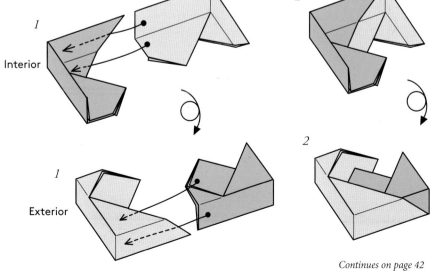

1 Interior

2

1 Exterior

2

Continues on page 42

Continued from page 42

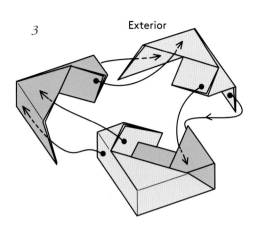

3 Exterior

Hanabishi

4

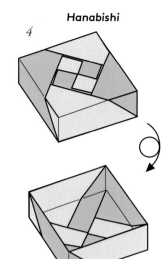

Hanahanabishi

4

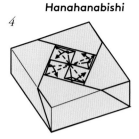

Open triangles and
press to flatten.

5

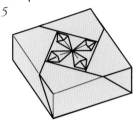

Square Box · *Yaehanabishi* Lid A, B

6 x 6 in (15 x 15 cm) sheets are standard

Here, the flower petals are doubled.

From step 8 on page 41

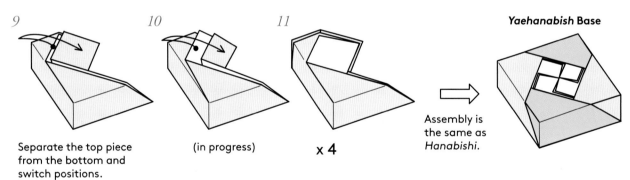

9

Separate the top piece
from the bottom and
switch positions.

10

(in progress)

11

x 4

Assembly is
the same as
Hanabishi.

Yaehanabish Base

Yaehanabishi A (View from above)

1

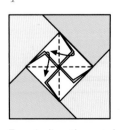

2

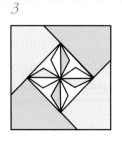

3

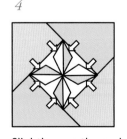

Try winding the petals with a
toothpick to curl them outward.

Yaehanabishi B

4

5

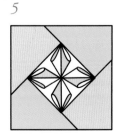

Slightly open the pockets where
the arrows are pointing

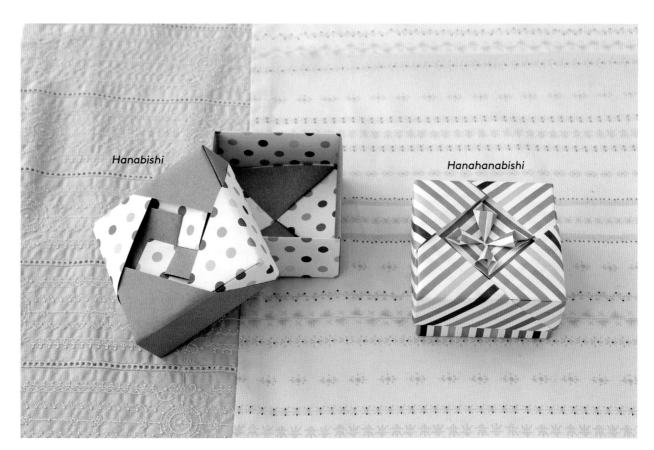

Hanabishi

Hanahanabishi

A with curled petals

Yaehanabishi A

Yaehanabishi B

Square Box Base 6 x 6 in (15 x 15 cm) sheets are standard

This is the same square box base from pages 36-43, made from paper that is equal to the size of the lid paper. Although this is a simple assembly, the layering provides extra sturdiness.

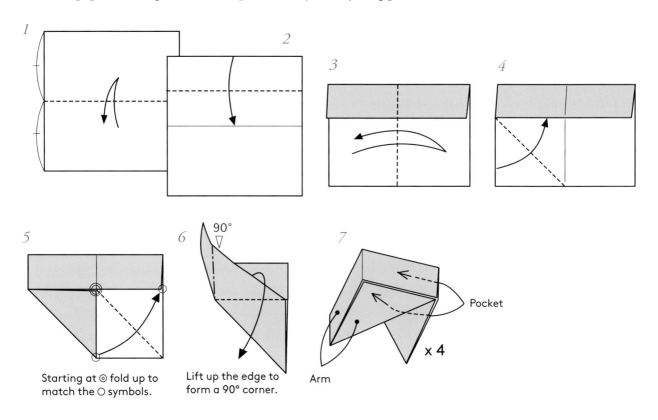

1 *2* *3* *4*

5
Starting at ⊚ fold up to match the ○ symbols.

6 90°
Lift up the edge to form a 90° corner.

7
Pocket
Arm
x 4

● **Assembly**

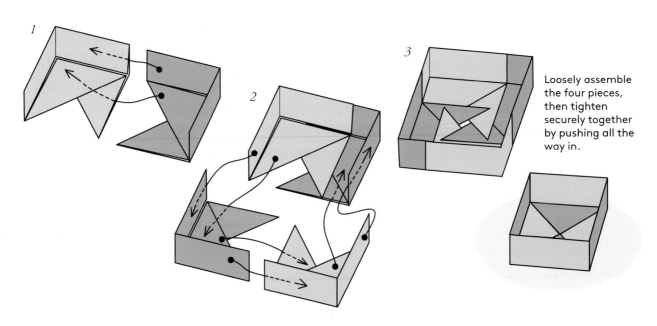

1 *2* *3*

Loosely assemble the four pieces, then tighten securely together by pushing all the way in.

"X" Partition 6 x 6 in (15 x 15 cm) sheets are standard

If the paper has the standard thickness of conventional origami paper, the partition can be made from paper that's the same size, but if the partition paper is thicker, trim the size by about $1/16$ in (1~2 mm).

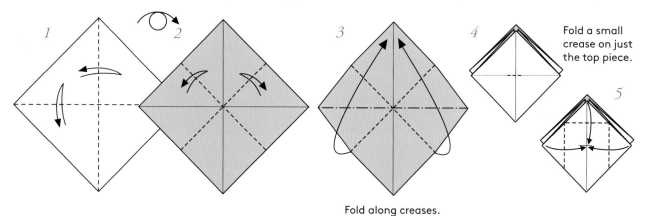

1

2

3

4 Fold a small crease on just the top piece.

5

Fold along creases.

6

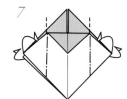
7

Reverse fold four sections.

8

Open and flip.

9

10

11

Keep the bottom triangle folded then pull forward to flatten.

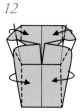

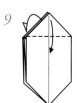

12

Stand up the sides.

13

Fold as though splitting it apart.

14

Place in base.

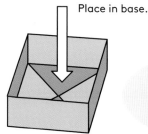

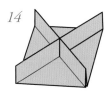

Modular Flower Roll Box

6 x 6 in (15 x 15 cm) sheets are standard

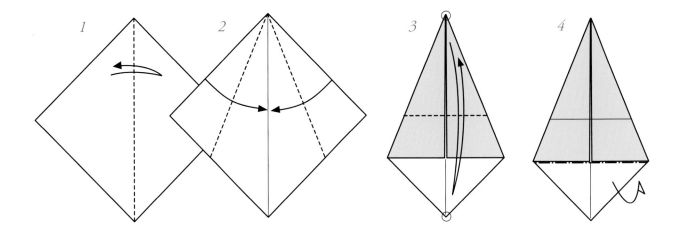

C

Lid 2¹/₂ x 2¹/₂ x 1 in
(6.2 x 6.2 x 2.3 cm)
(Does not include the
height of the flower)

Base 2¹/₄ x 2¹/₄ x 1⁷/₈ in
(5.7 x 5.7 x 4.7 cm)

Lid A with the inner colors
exposed and the tips curled

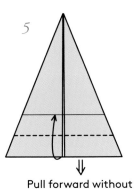

Pull forward without
folding the bottom.

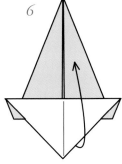

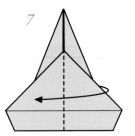

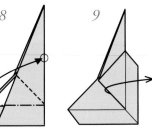

Fold in half.

Matching the ○ symbols
fold the top layer along
the dotted line shown.
Open to form a corner
with two sides.

Open.

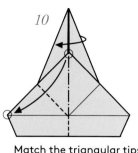

10

Match the triangular tips at the ○ symbols and fold to the edge, forming the same corner shape again.

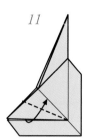

11

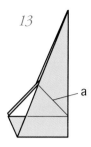

12

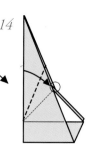

13

a

14

Fold to line "a" shown in step 13.

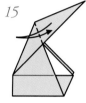

15

Crease along line shown.

16

17

Open and fold.

18

Restore.

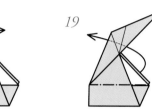

19

Open the bottom at a 90° angle, prop up the corner and sides and flatten the top.

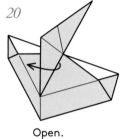

20

Open.

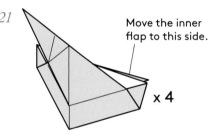

21

Move the inner flap to this side.

x 4

● **Assembly**

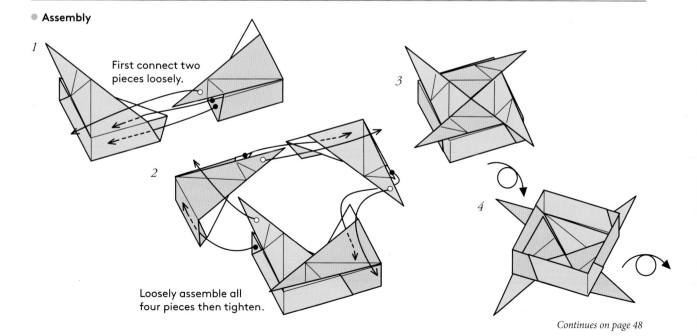

1

First connect two pieces loosely.

3

2

Loosely assemble all four pieces then tighten.

4

Continues on page 48

Modular Boxes From Multiple Square Sheets   47

Continued from page 47

Interior viewed from above

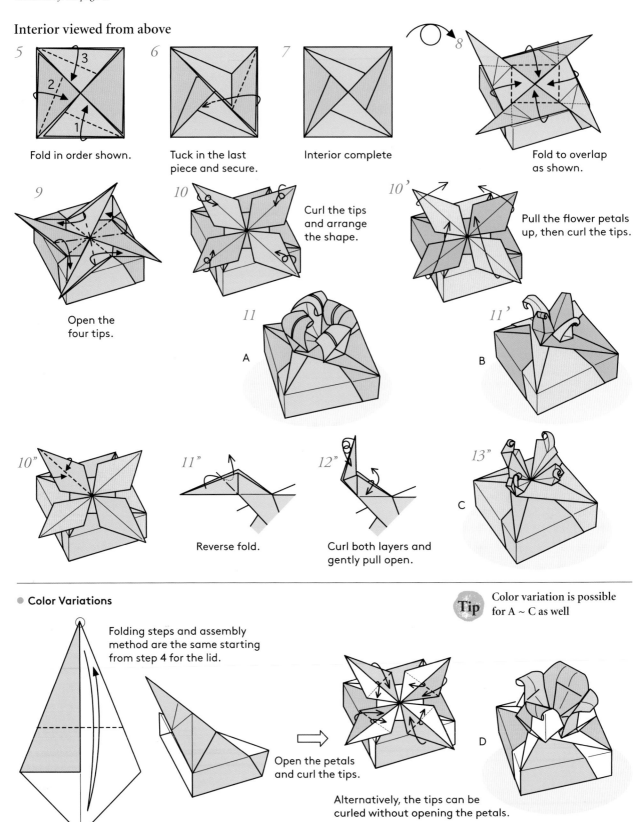

5 Fold in order shown.

6 Tuck in the last piece and secure.

7 Interior complete

8 Fold to overlap as shown.

9 Open the four tips.

10 Curl the tips and arrange the shape.

10' Pull the flower petals up, then curl the tips.

11 A

11' B

10"

11" Reverse fold.

12" Curl both layers and gently pull open.

13" C

● **Color Variations**

Tip Color variation is possible for A ~ C as well

Folding steps and assembly method are the same starting from step 4 for the lid.

Open the petals and curl the tips.

D

Alternatively, the tips can be curled without opening the petals.

Flower Roll Spiral Box 6 x 6 in (15 x 15 cm) sheets are standard

From step 15 on page 47

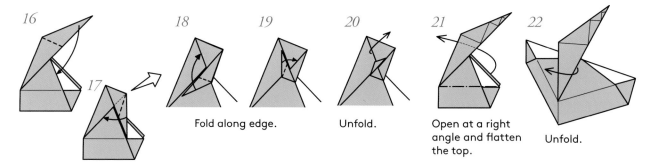

16

17

18
Fold along edge.

19
Unfold.

20

21
Open at a right angle and flatten the top.

22
Unfold.

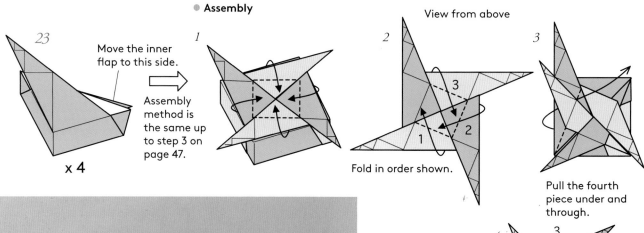

● **Assembly**

23

Move the inner flap to this side.

Assembly method is the same up to step 3 on page 47.

x 4

1

View from above

2
Fold in order shown.

3
Pull the fourth piece under and through.

4
Repeat to create a spiral effect.

Twist the tip to secure the spiral.

5

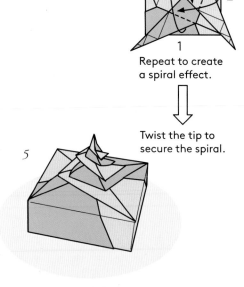

Flower Roll Base 6 x 6 in (15 x 15 cm) sheets are standard

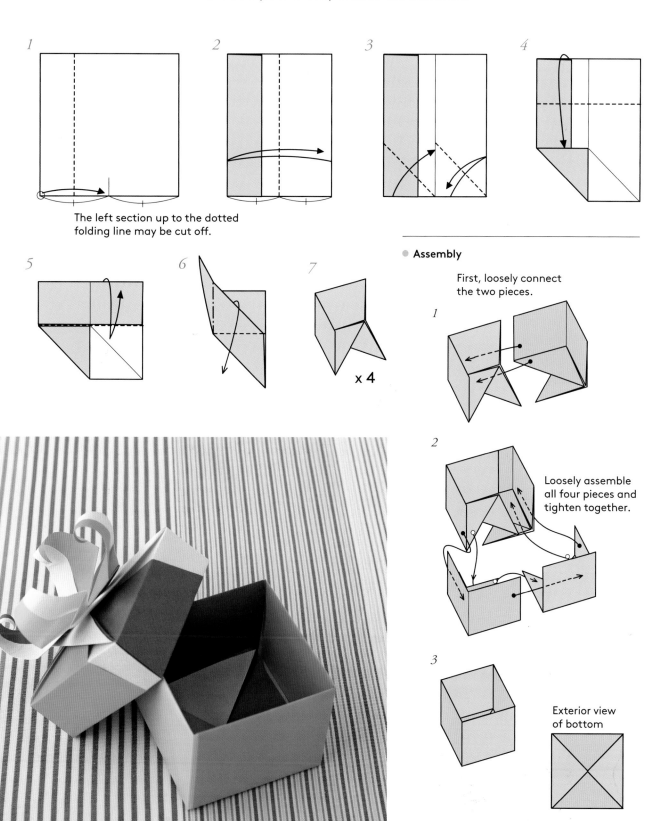

The left section up to the dotted folding line may be cut off.

x 4

● **Assembly**

First, loosely connect the two pieces.

Loosely assemble all four pieces and tighten together.

Exterior view of bottom

Hexagonal Pansy Box

6 x 6 in (15 x 15 cm) sheets are standard

Try folding the tips of the *Hanabishi* petals in different ways to get different looks.

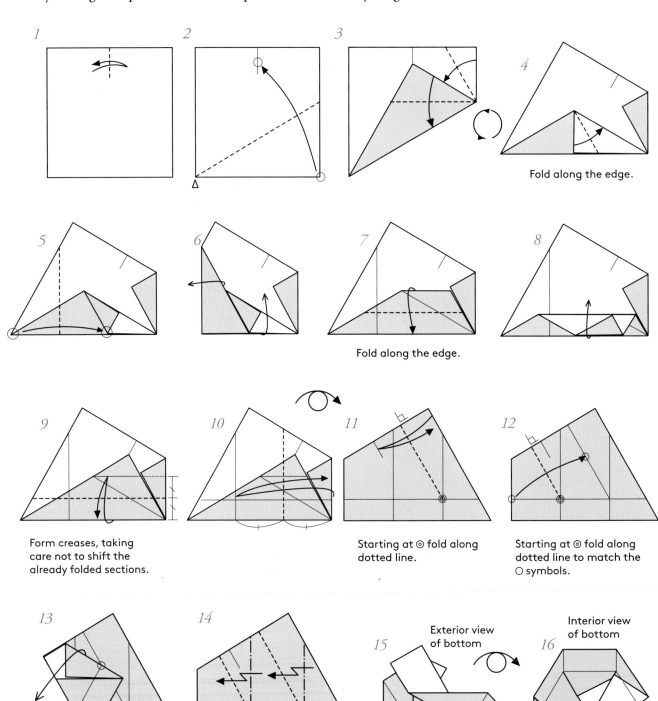

1

2

3

4

Fold along the edge.

5

6

7

Fold along the edge.

8

9

Form creases, taking care not to shift the already folded sections.

10

11

Starting at ⊚ fold along dotted line.

12

Starting at ⊚ fold along dotted line to match the ○ symbols.

13

Unfold.

14

Fold into flaps.

15

Exterior view of bottom

16

Interior view of bottom

x 3

Loosely assemble, then tighten
all three pieces securely together
by pushing all the way in.

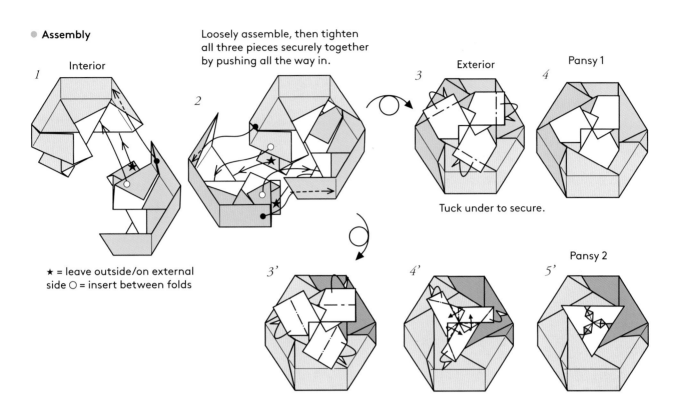

★ = leave outside/on external
side ○ = insert between folds

Tuck under to secure.

Pansy 1

Lid 4¹/₂ x 4¹/₂ x 1 in (11.5 x 11.5 x 2.6 cm)

Hexagonal Plain Box 1 and 2 6 x 6 in (15 x 15 cm) sheets are standard

There are two ways to assemble this type of box. The kind without any adornment is called *muji*, meaning "plain."

Start from step 10 on page 52.

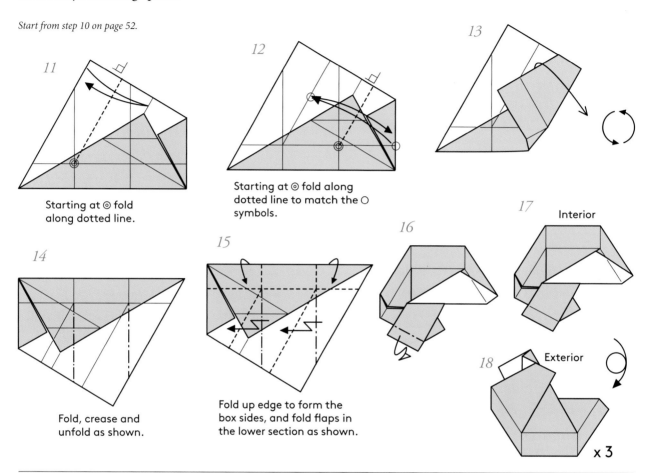

11 Starting at ◎ fold along dotted line.

12 Starting at ◎ fold along dotted line to match the ○ symbols.

13

14 Fold, crease and unfold as shown.

15 Fold up edge to form the box sides, and fold flaps in the lower section as shown.

16

17 Interior

18 Exterior

x 3

● **Assembly for Plain Hexagonal Box 1**

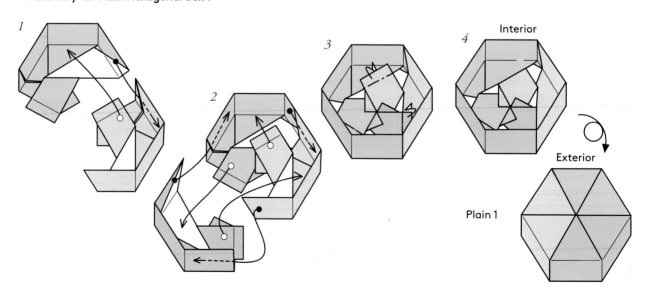

1

2

3

4 Interior

Plain 1

Exterior

● Assembly for Plain Hexagonal Box 2

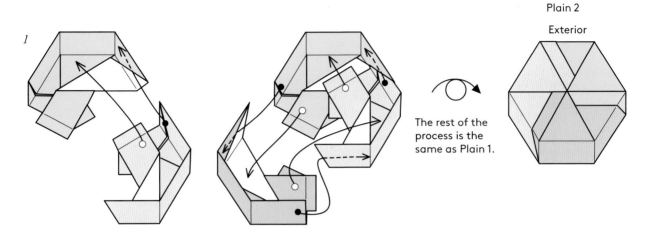

1

Plain 2
Exterior

The rest of the
process is the
same as Plain 1.

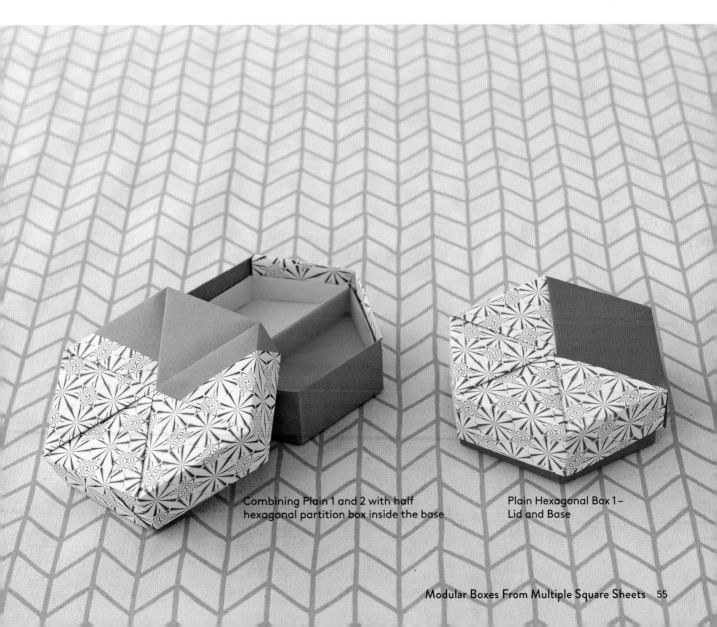

Combining Plain 1 and 2 with half
hexagonal partition box inside the base

Plain Hexagonal Box 1 –
Lid and Base

Hexagonal Box Base 6 x 6 in (15 x 15 cm) sheets are standard

We will start by folding a sheet to serve as a template.

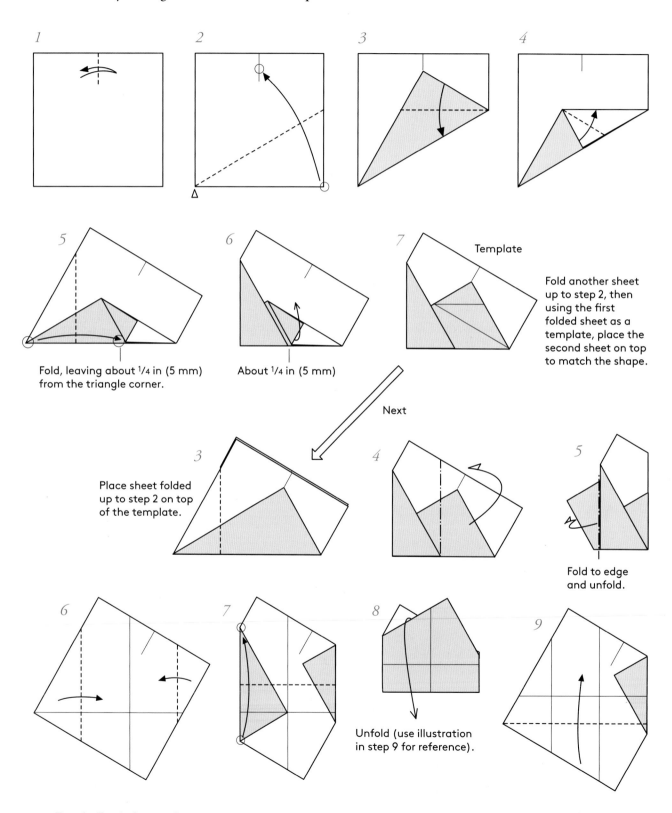

1

2

Δ

3

4

5

Fold, leaving about ¼ in (5 mm) from the triangle corner.

6

About ¼ in (5 mm)

7

Template

Fold another sheet up to step 2, then using the first folded sheet as a template, place the second sheet on top to match the shape.

Next

3

Place sheet folded up to step 2 on top of the template.

4

5

Fold to edge and unfold.

6

7

8

Unfold (use illustration in step 9 for reference).

9

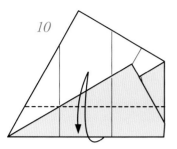

10

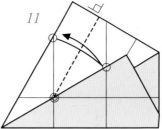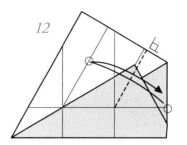

11

Starting at ◎ fold along
dotted line to match the ○
symbols.

12

Fold up to the ○ symbol.

13

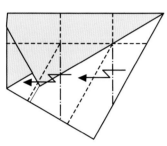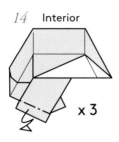

14 Interior

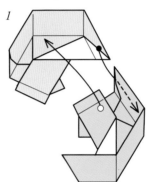

x 3

Tip The assembly method is the same as for the Plain
Hexagonal Box (page 54) and can be done in two ways.
Here we used the Plain 1 method.

● **Assembly for Plain 1**

1

2

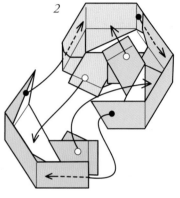

3

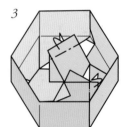

4

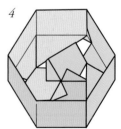

Exterior

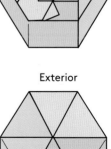

4³/₈ x 4³/₈ x 1¹/₈ in (11.2 x 11.2 x 3.1 cm)

Half Hexagonal Box

These partition boxes fit nicely into the Hexagonal Boxes on page 56. We recommend folding these using paper that's 6$\frac{1}{8}$ or 6$\frac{1}{4}$- in (15.5 or 16 cm) square.

1

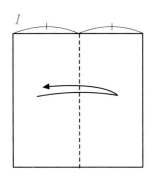

2

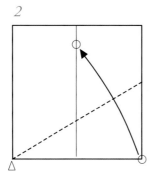

3

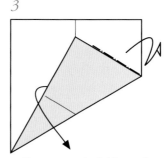

The mountain folds on the upper right and left should extend far enough to meet the vertical lines in step 6.

4

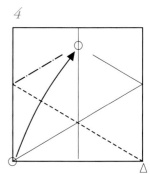

Starting at △ fold along dotted line to match the ○ symbols.

5

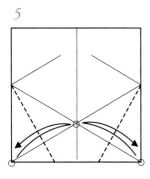

6

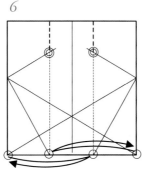

Match the ○ symbols and fold from ◎ to top edge.

7

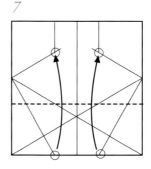

8

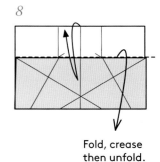

Fold, crease then unfold.

9

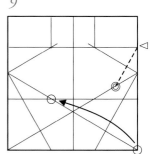

Match the ○ symbols and fold from △ to ◎ symbol.

10

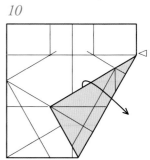

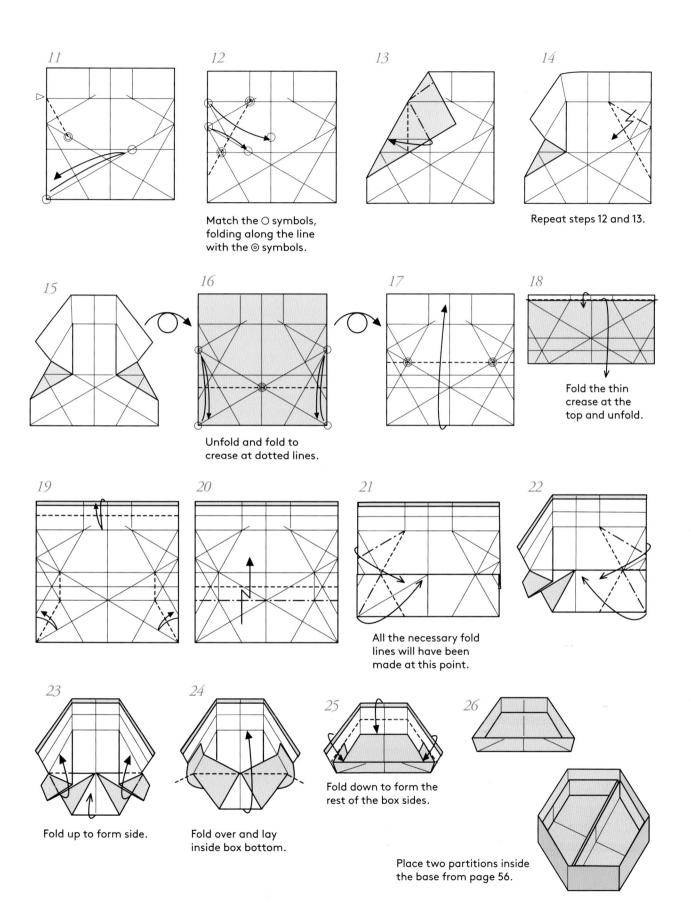

11 **12** Match the ○ symbols, folding along the line with the ⊙ symbols.

13 **14** Repeat steps 12 and 13.

15 **16** Unfold and fold to crease at dotted lines.

17 **18** Fold the thin crease at the top and unfold.

19 **20** **21** All the necessary fold lines will have been made at this point.

22

23 Fold up to form side.

24 Fold over and lay inside box bottom.

25 Fold down to form the rest of the box sides.

26 Place two partitions inside the base from page 56.

Rectangular Box Base

6 x 6 in (15 x 15 cm) sheets are standard

This surprisingly simple base involves two unit designs, and we will be making two of each.

Base : A

1

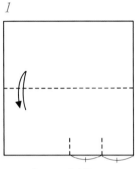

Create folding line as shown.

2

Crease the vertical line 1 shown above as both a mountain and valley fold; this will make step 4 easier.

3

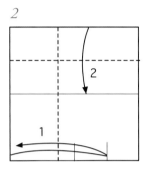

Starting at ◎ fold along dotted line to match the ○ symbols .

4

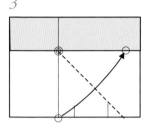

Fold down, then unfold and fold to create sides with a 90° corner.

5

Revert to step 4.

6

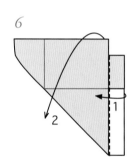

7

Fold while opening the right section to form a box side.

8

Lift and tuck into short side.

9

10 A

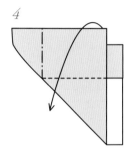

Interior

x 2

Exterior

Lid 4⁵/₈ x 3¹/₈ x 1in (11.8 x 8 x 2.7 cm)

Base B

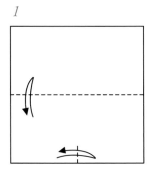

1

Create folding line as shown.

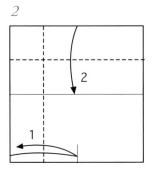

2

Crease the vertical line 1 shown above as both a mountain and valley fold; this will make step 5 easier.

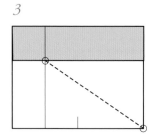

3

Create folding line as shown.

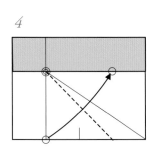

4

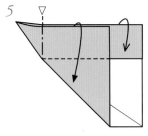

5

Fold over, then unfold and fold to create sides with a 90° corner.

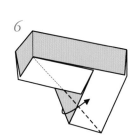

6

Fold along the line formed in step 3.

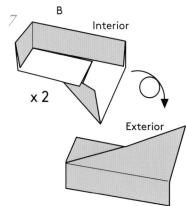

7

B   Interior

x 2

Exterior

● Assembly

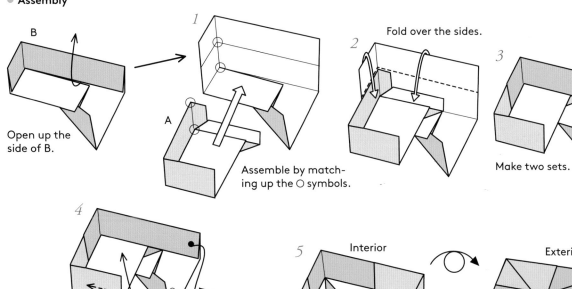

B

Open up the side of B.

1

A

Assemble by matching up the ○ symbols.

Fold over the sides.

2

3

Make two sets.

4

5

Interior

Exterior

Insert

An insert is an optional step that reinforces the box bottom and allows for a neater finish.

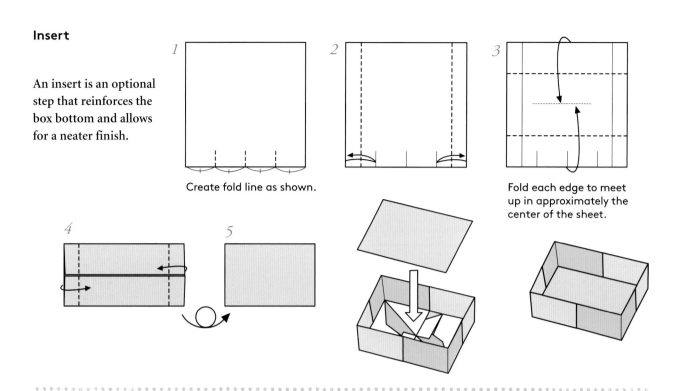

Create fold line as shown.

Fold each edge to meet up in approximately the center of the sheet.

Rectangular Box Lid 6 x 6 in (15 x 15 cm) sheets are standard

For the lid, the initial fold is slightly shifted to the left. The illustration is for reference but is not meant to be an exact representation. Adjust the fold depending on the thickness and width of your paper. For this project we will be using two types of paper.

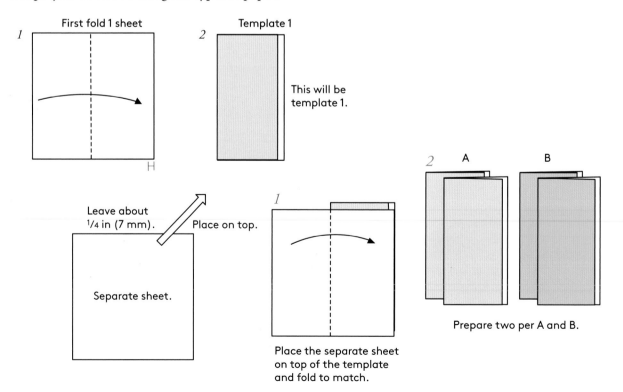

First fold 1 sheet

Template 1

This will be template 1.

Leave about 1/4 in (7 mm). Place on top.

Separate sheet.

Place the separate sheet on top of the template and fold to match.

Prepare two per A and B.

Using B, create template 2.

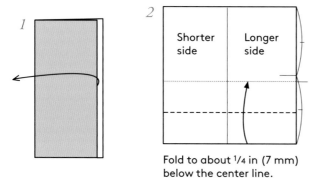

1

2
| Shorter side | Longer side |

Fold to about ¼ in (7 mm) below the center line.

3
This will be template 2.

Use this for B (page 64).

Lid : A

Tip
When matching a second sheet to the shape of a template, stagger the papers to make the process easier

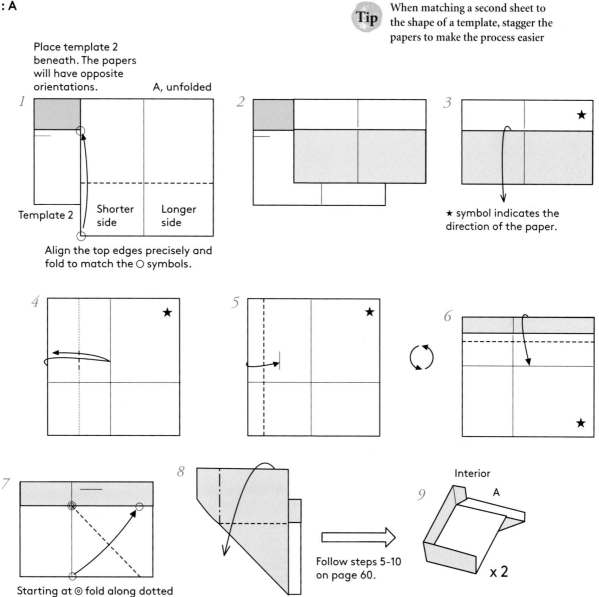

1

Place template 2 beneath. The papers will have opposite orientations.

A, unfolded

Template 2 | Shorter side | Longer side

Align the top edges precisely and fold to match the ○ symbols.

2

3

★ symbol indicates the direction of the paper.

4

5

6

7

Starting at ◎ fold along dotted line to match the ○ symbols.

8

Follow steps 5-10 on page 60.

9

Interior

A

x 2

Lid : B

Place unfolded B on top of template 2.

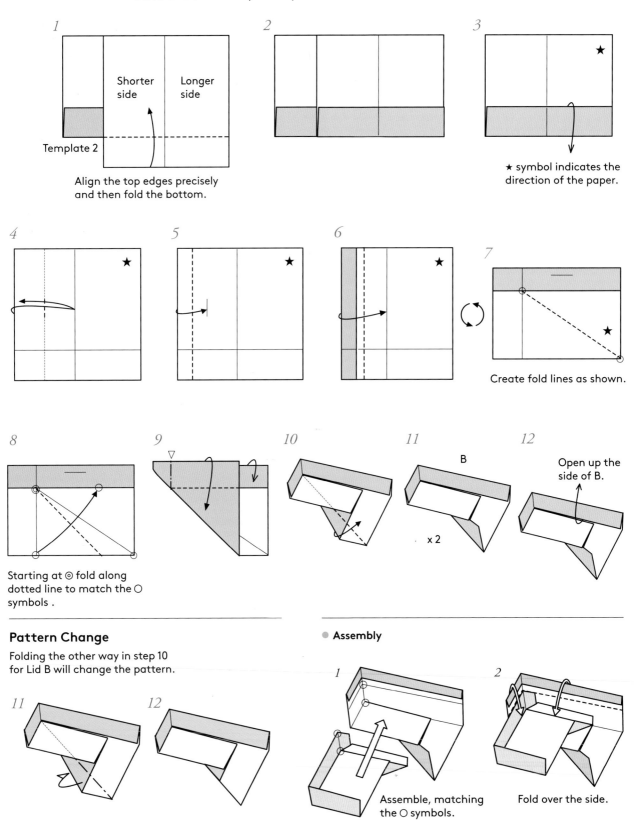

1

Shorter side

Longer side

Template 2

Align the top edges precisely and then fold the bottom.

2

3

★ symbol indicates the direction of the paper.

4

5

6

★

7

Create fold lines as shown.

8

Starting at ◎ fold along dotted line to match the ○ symbols .

9

10

11

B

x 2

12

Open up the side of B.

Pattern Change

Folding the other way in step 10 for Lid B will change the pattern.

11

12

● **Assembly**

1

Assemble, matching the ○ symbols.

2

Fold over the side.

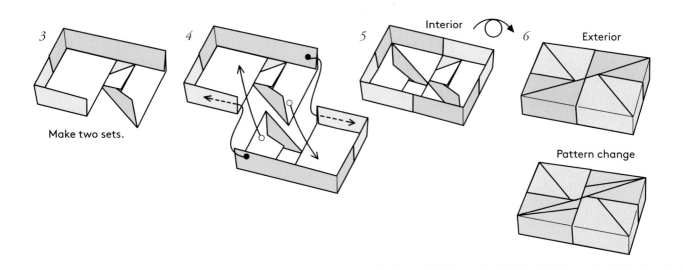

3

Make two sets.

4

5

Interior

6

Exterior

Pattern change

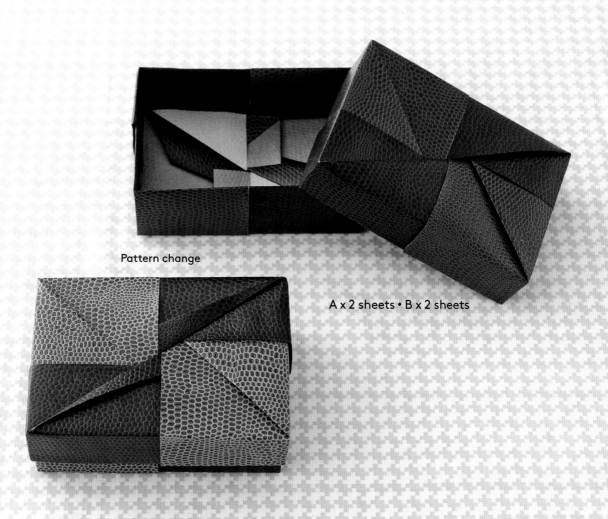

Pattern change

A x 2 sheets • B x 2 sheets

Skewed Hexagonal Box Base

5³/₄ x 5³/₄ in (14.3 x 14.3 cm) sheets are standard

The base for this box is made from a slightly smaller sheet than is used for the lid. Though not the most elegant solution, trimming the paper prevents forced folds and enables a more streamlined finish. Conventional store-bought origami paper may not be up to the multiple folds, so start by practicing on that and switching to a slightly thicker paper for the final version.

Base : A

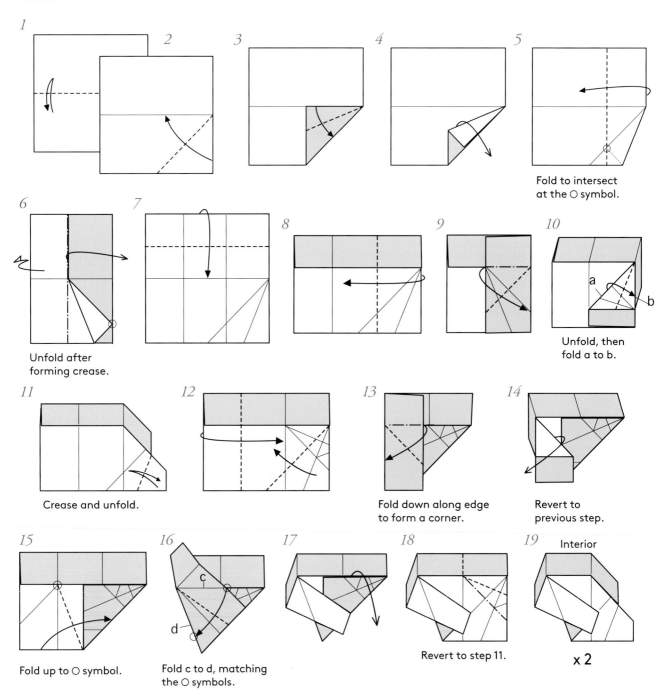

1

2

3

4

5

Fold to intersect
at the ○ symbol.

6

Unfold after
forming crease.

7

8

9

10

Unfold, then
fold a to b.

11

Crease and unfold.

12

13

Fold down along edge
to form a corner.

14

Revert to
previous step.

15

Fold up to ○ symbol.

16

Fold c to d, matching
the ○ symbols.

17

18

Revert to step 11.

19   Interior

x 2

Base : B

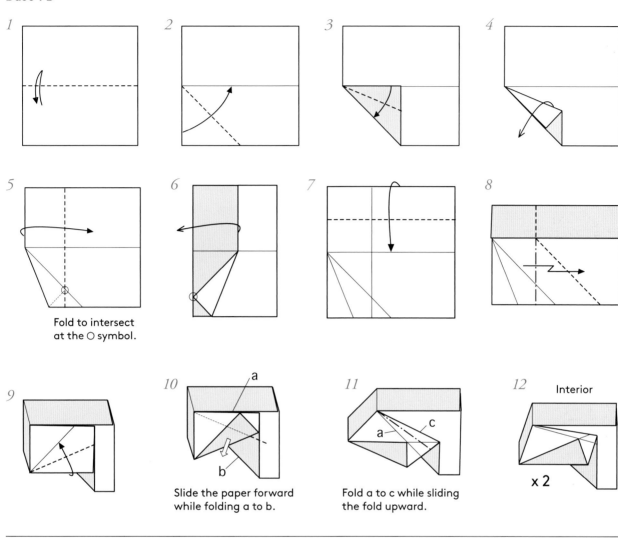

5 Fold to intersect at the ○ symbol.

10 Slide the paper forward while folding a to b.

11 Fold a to c while sliding the fold upward.

12 Interior

x 2

● **Assembly**

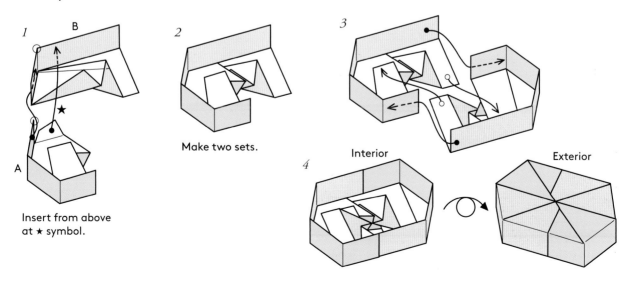

1 Insert from above at ★ symbol.

2 Make two sets.

4 Interior   Exterior

Skewed Hexagonal Box Lid 6 x 6 in (15 x 15 cm) sheets are standard

The lid is folded from a sheet that is larger than the base paper by about ¼ in (7 mm) per side.

Lid : A

Start from step 7 on page 66.

1
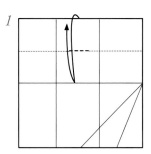

2
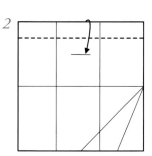

3
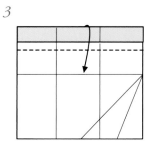

4
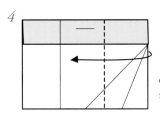

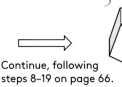

5
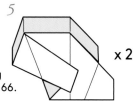 **x 2**

Continue, following
steps 8–19 on page 66.

Lid : B

Start from step 7 on page 67.

1
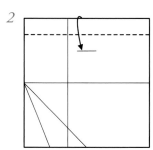

2
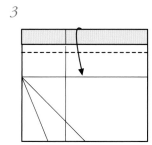

3

4
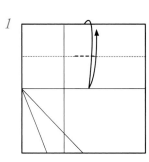

Continue,
following
steps 8-12
on page 67.

5
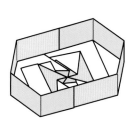 **x 2**

Assembly
method is
the same
as shown
on page 67.

Insert

*This step is optional, but adds strength to the
box and gives a cleaner look.*

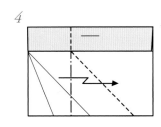

Measure the length "L" of
the base to determine the
longest side of the insert.

1
L
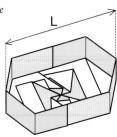

2
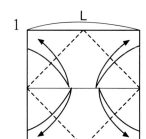

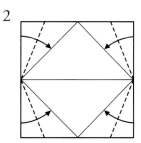

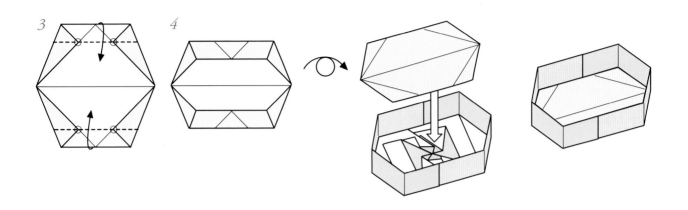

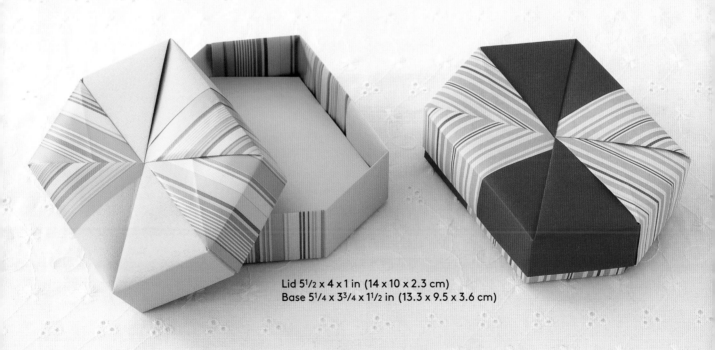

Lid 5¹/₂ x 4 x 1 in (14 x 10 x 2.3 cm)
Base 5¹/₄ x 3³/₄ x 1¹/₂ in (13.3 x 9.5 x 3.6 cm)

Barrel-Shaped Box Lid 6 x 6 in (15 x 15 cm) sheets are standard

This lid involves two kinds of unit (A, B) and we will make two of each.

Lid : A

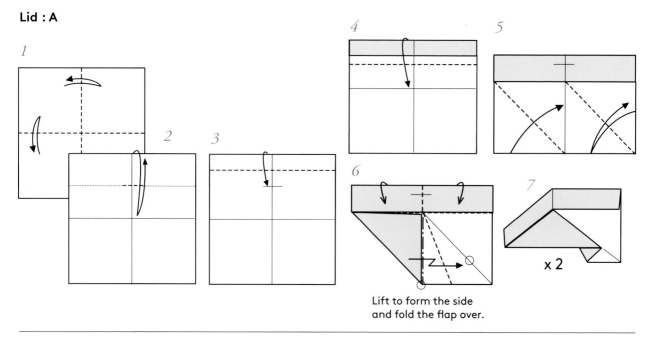

Lift to form the side
and fold the flap over.

Lid : B *Start from step 5 for unit A.*

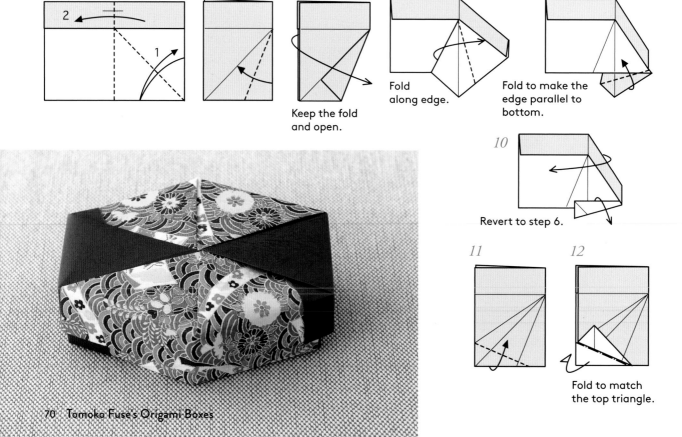

Keep the fold
and open.

Fold
along edge.

Fold to make the
edge parallel to
bottom.

Revert to step 6.

Fold to match
the top triangle.

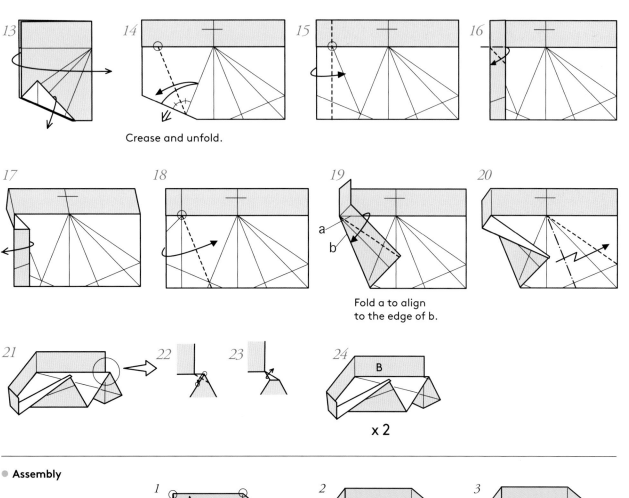

Crease and unfold.

Fold a to align
to the edge of b.

x 2

● **Assembly**

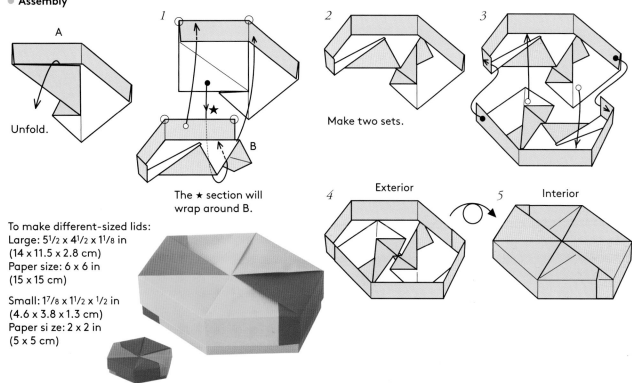

A

Unfold.

The ★ section will
wrap around B.

Make two sets.

Exterior

Interior

To make different-sized lids:
Large: 5¹/₂ x 4¹/₂ x 1¹/₈ in
(14 x 11.5 x 2.8 cm)
Paper size: 6 x 6 in
(15 x 15 cm)

Small: 1⁷/₈ x 1¹/₂ x ¹/₂ in
(4.6 x 3.8 x 1.3 cm)
Paper si ze: 2 x 2 in
(5 x 5 cm)

Barrel-Shaped Box and Lid 6 x 6 in (15 x 15 cm) sheets are standard

The base is folded in a way that makes it smaller than the lid. If the paper for A is thick, you may want to trim away a little on each side.

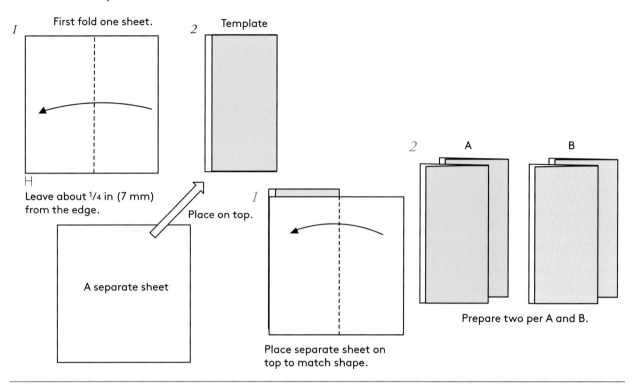

1 First fold one sheet.

Leave about ¼ in (7 mm) from the edge.

A separate sheet

Place on top.

2 Template

1 Place separate sheet on top to match shape.

2 A B

Prepare two per A and B.

Base : A

1 *2* *3* *4*

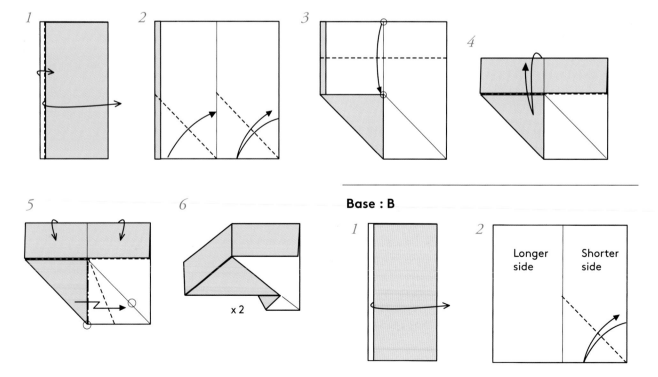

5 *6* x 2

Base : B

1 *2* Longer side   Shorter side

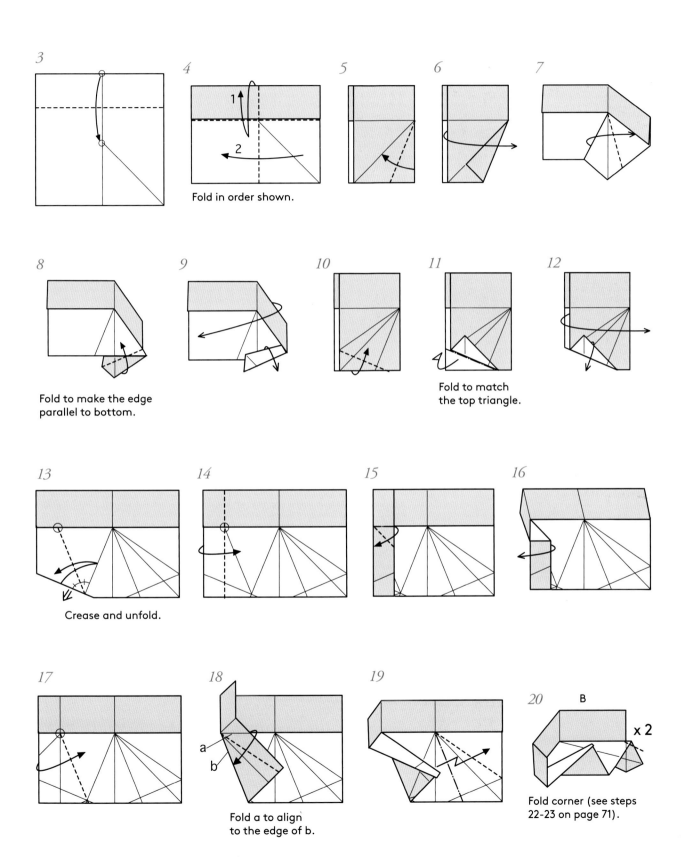

3

4

Fold in order shown.

5

6

7

8

9

Fold to make the edge
parallel to bottom.

10

11

Fold to match
the top triangle.

12

13

Crease and unfold.

14

15

16

17

18

Fold a to align
to the edge of b.

a

b

19

20

B

x 2

Fold corner (see steps
22-23 on page 71).

● Assembly

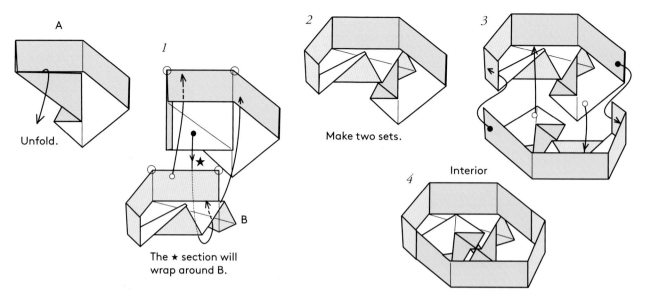

A

Unfold.

1

The ★ section will
wrap around B.

B

2

Make two sets.

3

4 Interior

Part 3
Modular Boxes From Rectangular Sheets

Around the world, rectangular paper is more common than square paper. This chapter includes various box units that can be folded from rectangular paper. Many folding methods used for square paper are easily adaptable to rectangular origami sheets. This chapter is filled with festive boxes made from these units.

Octagonal Flower Box •
Hananira (Ipheion)
Page 82

Base Partition
Page 86

Hexagonal Flower Box
Page 88

Triangle Partition
Page 92

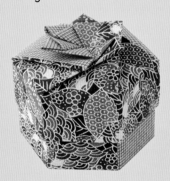

Hexagonal Flower Box
(From a vertical rectangle)
Page 93

Hexagonal Flower Box
(From a square)
Page 93

Octagonal Flower Box •
Mukuge (Hibiscus)
Page 81

Square Box • *Chomusubi*
(Butterfly Knot)
Page 76

Square Box • *Kongo-gumi*
(Spiral Braid)
Page 77

A Square Box Lid From a Rectangular Sheet

Cut a sheet of A4 paper in half. Alternatively, cut 8½ x 6-inch sheets from US letter or legal-size paper (8½ x 11 / 8½ x 14 inches).

This can be considered the standard for folding a square box from a rectangular sheet of paper. This project is great for beginners unfamiliar with modular origami. Rectangular paper offers a lot of flexibility in terms of ratio.

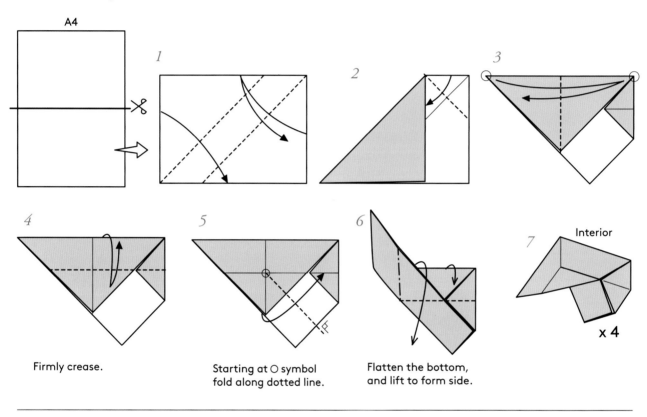

A4

1

2

3

4

Firmly crease.

5

Starting at ○ symbol fold along dotted line.

6

Flatten the bottom, and lift to form side.

7

Interior

x 4

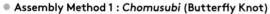

● **Assembly Method 1 : *Chomusubi* (Butterfly Knot)**

Tip The pointed end of the unit will be the "arm" to insert. See pages 37-38 for reference.

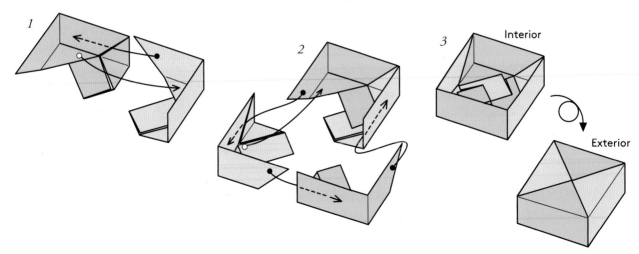

1

2

3

Interior

Exterior

Tip Reverse the arm and pocket in Assembly Method 1. Please see pages 37-38 for reference.

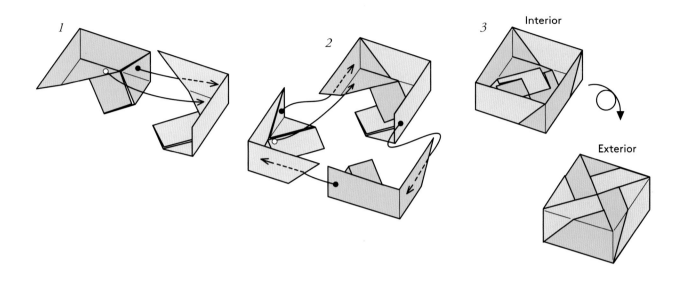

1

2

3 Interior

Exterior

● **Assembly Method 3 : *Kongo-gumi* (Spiral Braid)**

Tip As shown below, this unit has pockets on both sides so pieces can be inserted on either side.

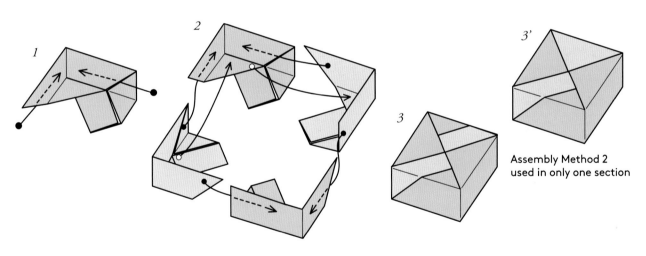

1

2

3

3'

Assembly Method 2 used in only one section

● **Color Variations**

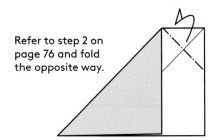

Refer to step 2 on page 76 and fold the opposite way.

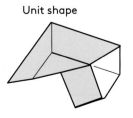

Unit shape

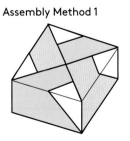

Assembly Method 1

Chomusubi (Butterfly Knot)

Windmill

Kongo-gumi (Spiral Braid)

Color Variations

A Square Box Base From a Rectangular Sheet

Cut a sheet of A4 paper in half. Alternatively, cut 8½ x 6-inch sheets from US letter or legal-size paper (8½ x 11/8½ x 14 inches).

Whereas the lid was made from a horizontal sheet, the base is folded from the vertical orientation. We'll start by creating a template.

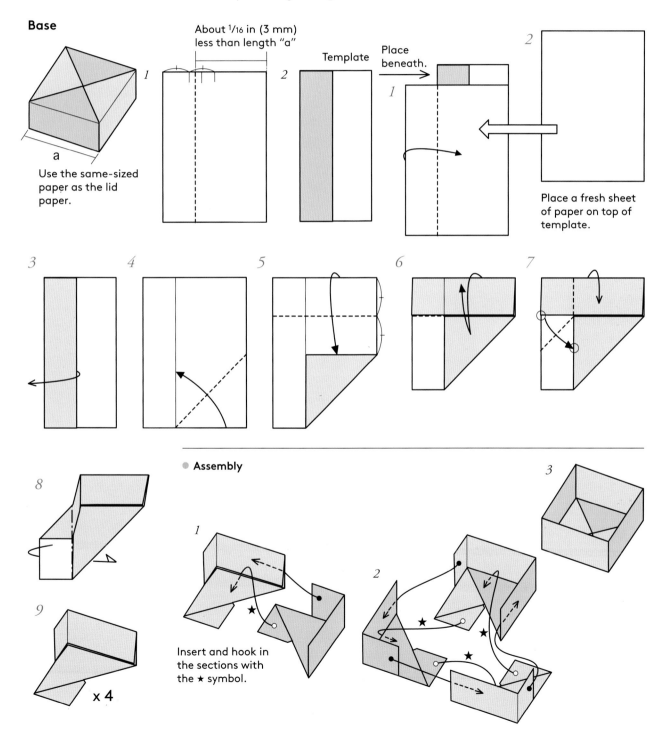

Base

Use the same-sized paper as the lid paper.

About 1/16 in (3 mm) less than length "a"

Template

Place beneath.

Place a fresh sheet of paper on top of template.

● Assembly

Insert and hook in the sections with the ★ symbol.

x 4

Octagonal *Hanamizuki* and *Mukuge* Flower Boxes

Cut A4 paper into quarters. Alternatively, cut sheets of 4¼ x 6 inches from US letter or legal-size paper (8½ x 11 / 8½ x 14 inches).

The octagonal box is sturdy and easy to construct and the lid's flower petals can be arranged in a variety of ways.

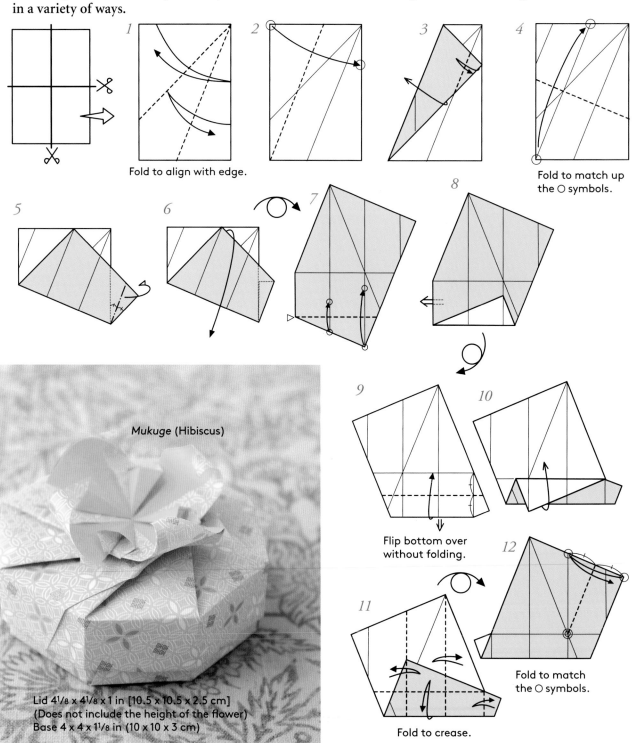

1 Fold to align with edge.

4 Fold to match up the ○ symbols.

9 Flip bottom over without folding.

11 Fold to crease.

12 Fold to match the ○ symbols.

Mukuge (Hibiscus)

Lid 4⅛ x 4⅛ x 1 in [10.5 x 10.5 x 2.5 cm] (Does not include the height of the flower)
Base 4 x 4 x 1⅛ in (10 x 10 x 3 cm)

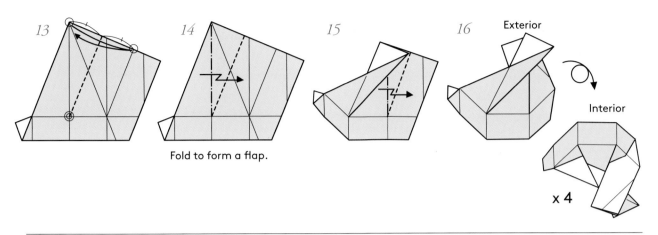

13 *14* *15* *16*

Exterior

Interior

Fold to form a flap.

x 4

● **Assembly**

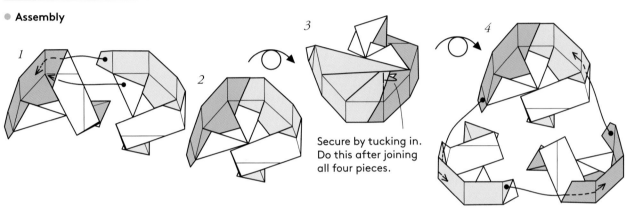

1 *2* *3* *4*

Secure by tucking in.
Do this after joining
all four pieces.

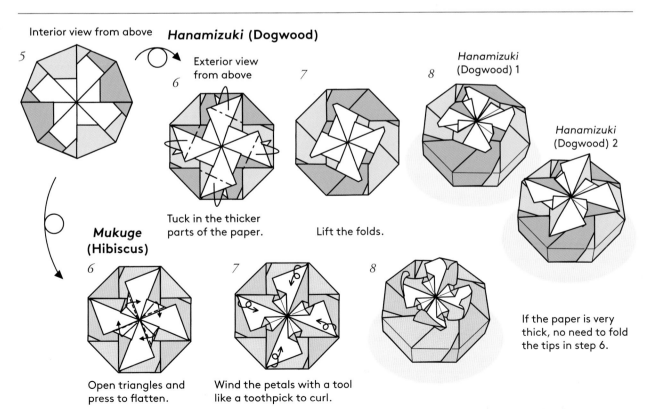

Interior view from above **Hanamizuki (Dogwood)**

5

Exterior view
from above

6 *7* *8* *Hanamizuki
(Dogwood) 1*

*Hanamizuki
(Dogwood) 2*

Tuck in the thicker
parts of the paper.

Lift the folds.

**Mukuge
(Hibiscus)**

6 *7* *8*

Open triangles and
press to flatten.

Wind the petals with a tool
like a toothpick to curl.

If the paper is very
thick, no need to fold
the tips in step 6.

Octagonal *Hananira* and *Senno* Flower Boxes

Lid: C *Start from step 13 on page 81*

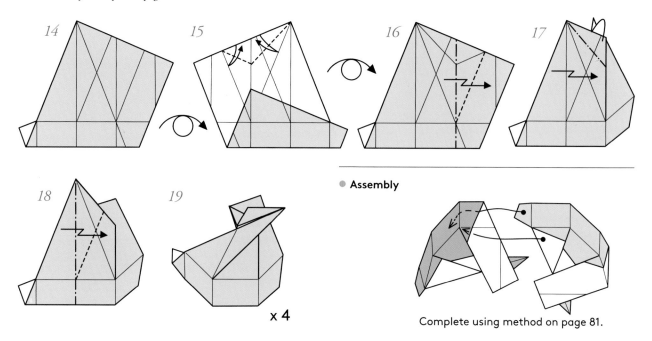

● **Assembly**

Complete using method on page 81.

x 4

Hananira (Ipheion)

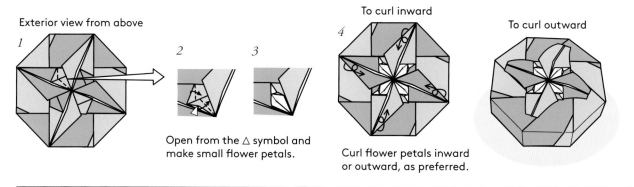

Exterior view from above

Open from the △ symbol and make small flower petals.

To curl inward

To curl outward

Curl flower petals inward or outward, as preferred.

Senno (Lychnis) *Start from step 15 of the* Hananira *(Ipheion) instructions.*

As shown on page 81

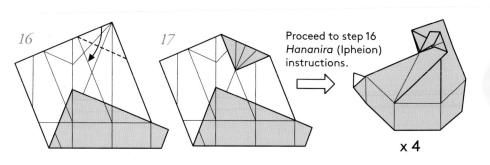

Proceed to step 16 *Hananira* (Ipheion) instructions.

x 4

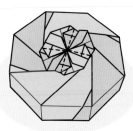

Lift up small folds or use the same method as *Hananira* (Ipheion).

Hanamizuki (Dogwood) 1

Hanamizuki (Dogwood) 2

Senno (Lychnis)

Octagonal Flower Box Base From Rectangular Sheets

Cut A4 paper into quarters. Alternatively, cut sheets of 4¼ x 6 inches from US letter or legal-size paper (8½ x 11 / 8½ x 14 inches).

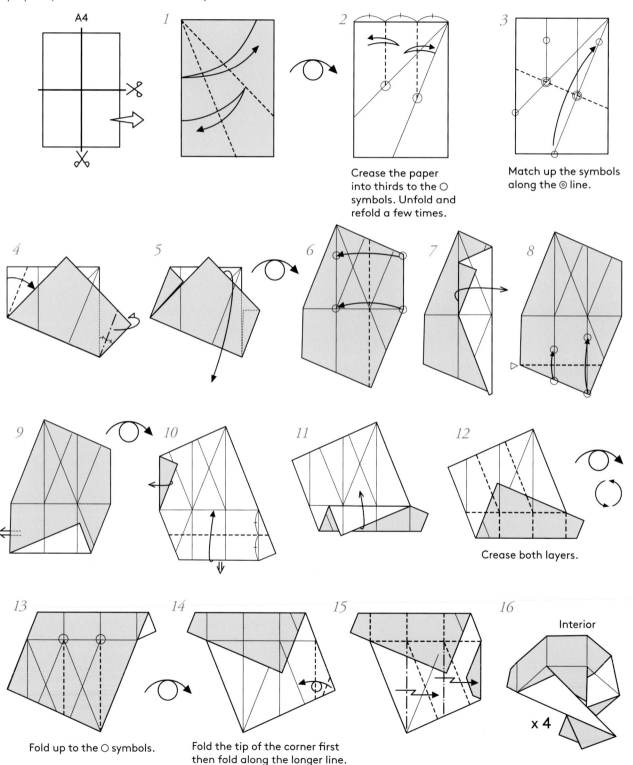

2 Crease the paper into thirds to the ○ symbols. Unfold and refold a few times.

3 Match up the symbols along the ◎ line.

12 Crease both layers.

13 Fold up to the ○ symbols.

14 Fold the tip of the corner first then fold along the longer line.

16 Interior

x 4

Assembly

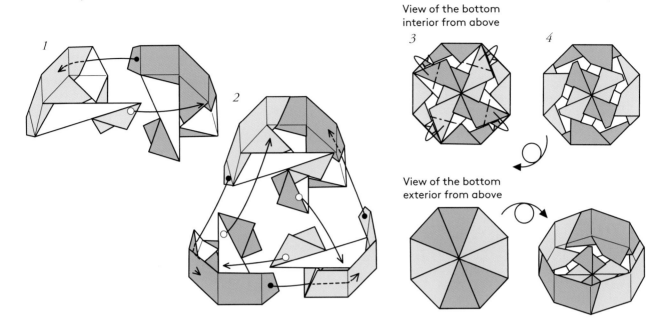

1

2

View of the bottom interior from above

3

4

View of the bottom exterior from above

Deep Box

Tip Folding along the dotted line shown below will produce a deep base.

From step 8 on page 84

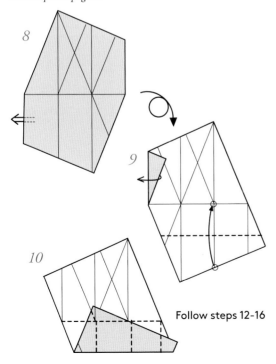

8

9

10

Follow steps 12-16

Octagonal Flower Insert With Partition From Rectangular Sheets

Cut A4 paper into quarters. Alternatively, cut 4¼ x 6-inch sheets from US letter or legal-size paper (8½ x 11 / 8½ x 14 inches)

The perfect partition for the Octagonal Flower Box. Adjust by the trimming the width depending on the thickness of the paper.

Use paper that is the same size as the one used for the Octagonal Flower Box.

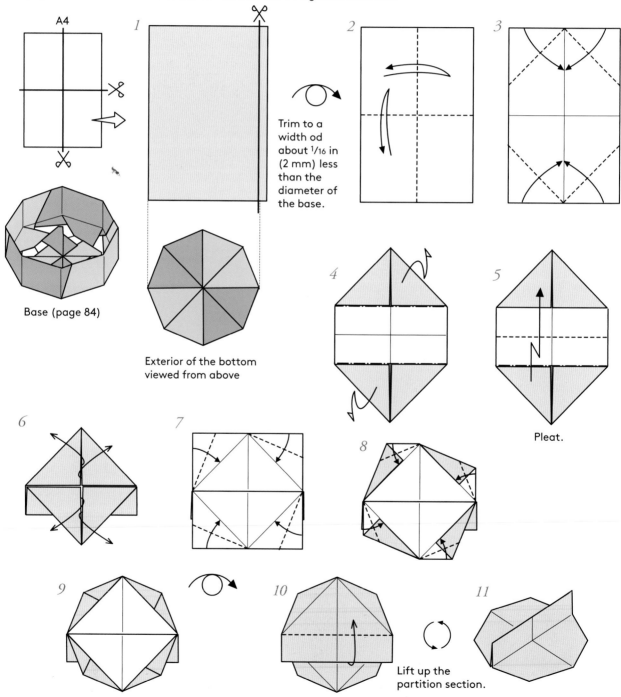

A4

1

Trim to a width od about ¹⁄₁₆ in (2 mm) less than the diameter of the base.

Base (page 84)

Exterior of the bottom viewed from above

2

3

4

5

Pleat.

6

7

8

9

10

Lift up the partition section.

11

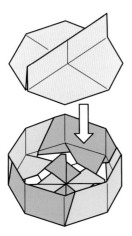
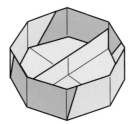

Octagonal Flower Box *Hananira* (Ipheion) and Partition

Hexagonal Flower Box Lid From Rectangular Sheets
Cut A4 copy paper in half. Alternatively, cut 8½ x 6-inch sheets from US letter or legal-size (8½ x 11 / 8½ x 14 inches).

Although the standard box uses A4 paper cut in half, any rectangular paper will do, including a square shape. (See page 96 for reference)

A4

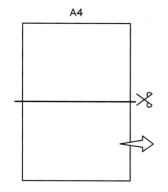

1

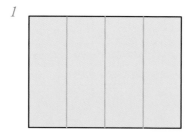

Use both mountain and valley folds for red lines shown (for each, make a mountain fold, then reverse it with a valley fold).

2

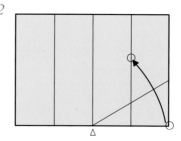

Fold along the △ symbol line, matching the ○ symbols.

3

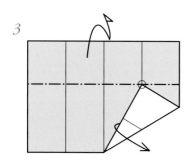

Fold to the ○ symbol.

4

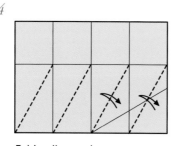

Fold a diagonal crease.

5

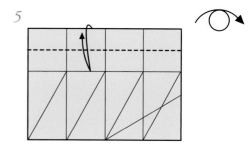

6

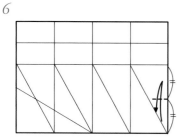

Create a small horizontal fold.

7

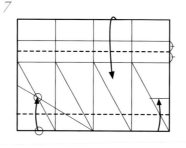

8

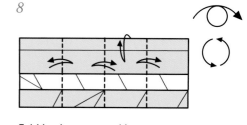

Fold both upper and lower layers together.

9

View of the two folds completed

10

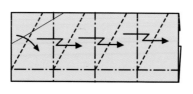

Create overlapping folds.

11

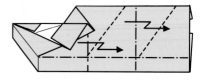

Example of two of the overlapping folds completed

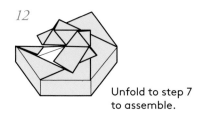

12

Unfold to step 7 to assemble.

13

Interior

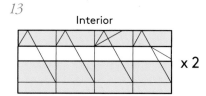

× 2

● **Assembly**

1

Interior

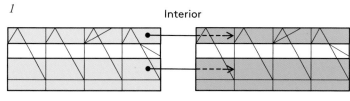

Insert up to the first line on the right.

2

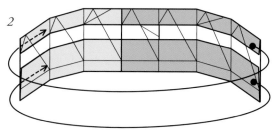

Connect into a loop

3

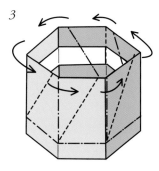

Press in and collapse the folds. Twist and flatten the top.

4

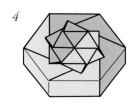

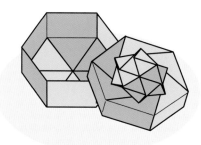

4'

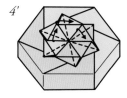

5'

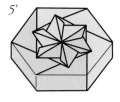

Alternatively, fold up the petals for added expressiveness.

Tips for Assembly

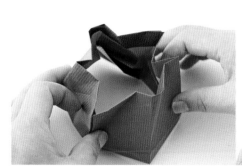

1. Pressing in and collapsing the folds

2. Twisting the folds

3. Pressing down the twisted folds

Raised folds (or petals)
and triangle partition

Flat folds (or petals)

Lid 4$^{1}/_{8}$ x 4$^{1}/_{8}$ x $^{5}/_{8}$ in (10.5 x 10.5 x 1.5 cm)
Base 4 x 4 x 1$^{1}/_{8}$ in (10 x 10 x 3 cm)

Hexagonal Flower Box Base From Rectangular Sheets

For the base, we'll reduce the width of the paper a little. Adjust the fold depending on the thickness of the paper.

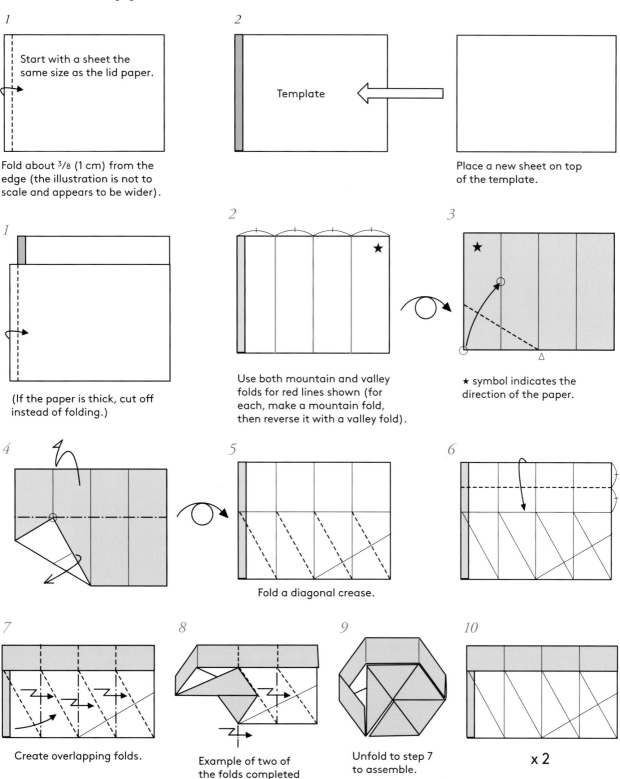

1

Start with a sheet the same size as the lid paper.

Fold about 3/8 (1 cm) from the edge (the illustration is not to scale and appears to be wider).

2

Template

Place a new sheet on top of the template.

1

(If the paper is thick, cut off instead of folding.)

2

Use both mountain and valley folds for red lines shown (for each, make a mountain fold, then reverse it with a valley fold).

3

★ symbol indicates the direction of the paper.

4

5

Fold a diagonal crease.

6

7

Create overlapping folds.

8

Example of two of the folds completed

9

Unfold to step 7 to assemble.

10

x 2

● Assembly

1

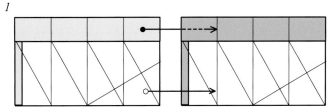

Insert up to the first line on the right.

2

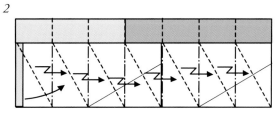

Insert up to the first line on the right.

The same base viewed from different angles.

The same base viewed from different angles.

3

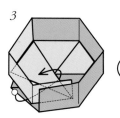

Tuck top piece under.

4

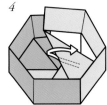

Switch positions by swinging the bottom up to the top.

5

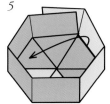

Gently lift up.

6

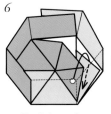

Tuck into the fold below.

7

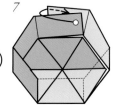

Insert one end of the side into the other.

8

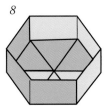

Triangle Partition

Tip This is just one of many ideas for making an easy partition. Take a long sheet of paper, fold it into a triangle and fit into the Hexagonal Box.

1

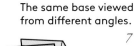

Fold a width that is about 1/16 in (1~2 mm) less than the diameter of the base and fold in half lengthwise.

Segment for glue

2

3

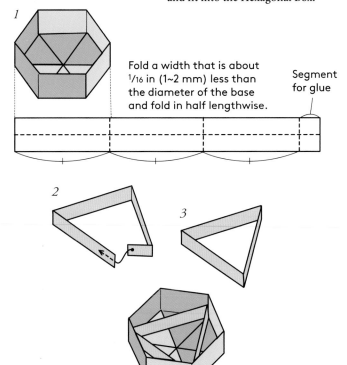

Octagonal Flower Box Lid Using Paper With Different Proportions 6 x 6 in (15 x 15 cm) sheets are standard

You can change the paper ratio and still fold an Octagonal Flower Box. The more vertical the paper, the deeper the box will be.

Using a square sheet of paper

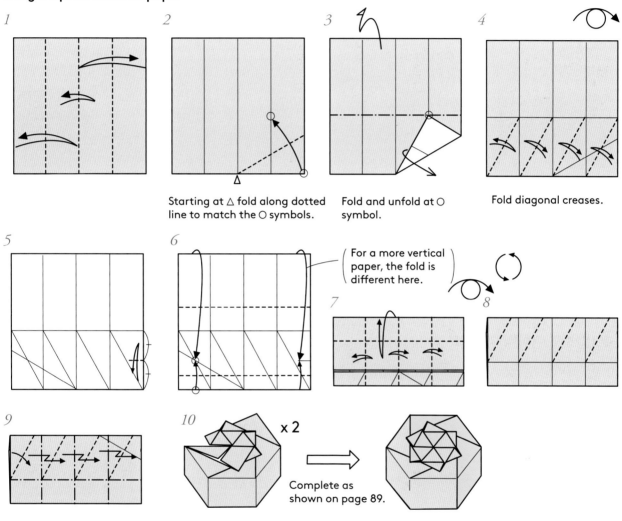

1

2

Starting at △ fold along dotted line to match the ○ symbols.

3

Fold and unfold at ○ symbol.

4

Fold diagonal creases.

5

6

For a more vertical paper, the fold is different here.

7

8

9

10

x 2

Complete as shown on page 89.

Using a vertical rectangular sheet

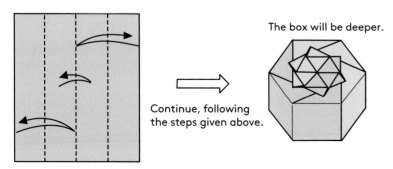

The box will be deeper.

Continue, following the steps given above.

Octagonal Flower Box Base Using Paper With Different Proportions 6 x 6 in (15 x 15 cm) sheets are standard

Using a square sheet

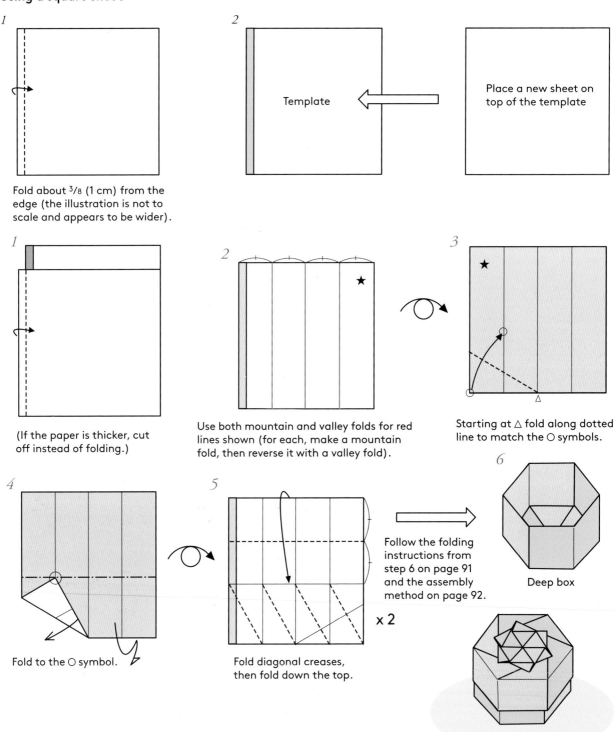

1

Fold about 3/8 (1 cm) from the edge (the illustration is not to scale and appears to be wider).

2

Template

Place a new sheet on top of the template

1

(If the paper is thicker, cut off instead of folding.)

2

Use both mountain and valley folds for red lines shown (for each, make a mountain fold, then reverse it with a valley fold).

3

Starting at △ fold along dotted line to match the ○ symbols.

4

Fold to the ○ symbol.

5

Fold diagonal creases, then fold down the top.

x 2

Follow the folding instructions from step 6 on page 91 and the assembly method on page 92.

6

Deep box

Lid 3¹/₈ x 3¹/₈ x ⁷/₈ in (8 x 8 x 2.2 cm)
Base 3 x 3 x 1⁵/₈ in (7.5 x 7.5 x 4.2 cm)

Folded from a vertical
rectangular sheet

Folded from a square sheet
Lid 2³/₄ x 2³/₄ x 1¹/₈ in (6.8 x 6.8 x 3 cm)
Base 2¹/₂ x 2¹/₂ x 1³/₄ in (6.2 x 6.2 x 4.5 cm)

ABOUT TUTTLE
"Books to Span the East and West"

Our core mission at Tuttle Publishing is to create books which bring people together one page at a time. Tuttle was founded in 1832 in the small New England town of Rutland, Vermont (USA). Our fundamental values remain as strong today as they were then—to publish best-in-class books informing the English-speaking world about the countries and peoples of Asia. The world has become a smaller place today and Asia's economic, cultural and political influence has expanded, yet the need for meaningful dialogue and information about this diverse region has never been greater. Since 1948, Tuttle has been a leader in publishing books on the cultures, arts, cuisines, languages and literatures of Asia. Our authors and photographers have won numerous awards and Tuttle has published thousands of books on subjects ranging from martial arts to paper crafts. We welcome you to explore the wealth of information available on Asia at www.tuttlepublishing.com.

Published by Tuttle Publishing, an imprint of Periplus Editions (HK) Ltd.

www.tuttlepublishing.com

ISBN 978-0-8048-5006-3

Hako no Origami (NV70177)
Copyright © 2013 by Tomoko Fuse/NIHON VOGUE-SHA
Photographer: Noriaki Moriya
All rights reserved.
English translation rights arranged with NIHON VOGUE Corp.
through Japan UNI Agency, Inc., Tokyo

Translation ©2018 Periplus Editions (HK) Ltd.
Translated from Japanese by Sanae Ishida

Staff:
Book Design | Fumie Terayama
Photography | Noriaki Moriya
Assistant Editor | Miku Koizumi, anga
Editor | Keisuke Morioka and Yukari Hiwasa

First Edition
22 21 20 19 18   5 4 3 2 1   1712RR
Printed in China

Distributed by

North America, Latin America & Europe
Tuttle Publishing
364 Innovation Drive, North Clarendon, VT 05759-9436 U.S.A.
Tel: 1 (802) 773-8930 | Fax: 1 (802) 773-6993
info@tuttlepublishing.com
www.tuttlepublishing.com

Asia Pacific
Berkeley Books Pte Ltd
61 Tai Seng Avenue #02-12, Singapore 534167
Tel: (65) 6280-1330 | Fax: (65) 6280-6290
inquiries@periplus.com.sg
www.periplus.com

Japan
Tuttle Publishing
Yaekari Building, 3F, 5-4-12 Osaki
Shinagawa-ku, Tokyo 141-0032
Tel: (81) 3 5437-0171 | Fax: (81) 3 5437-0755
sales@tuttle.co.jp
www.tuttle.co.jp

Indonesia
PT Java Books Indonesia
Jl. Rawa Gelam IV No. 9
Kawasan Industri Pulogadung
Jakarta 13930
Tel: (62) 21 4682-1088 | Fax: (62) 21 461-0206
crm@periplus.co.id
www.periplus.com